Annotated Teacher's Edition

STRATEGIES FOR READING

Avenues

by Lana Costantini

ISBN 0-8454-2537-4

CONTINENTAL PRESS
Elizabethtown, PA 17022

Table of Contents

Introducing *Strategies for Reading*

About the Series

Strategies for Reading is a supplemental program designed to help students read actively, think critically, and communicate effectively. High-interest, theme-related narratives from the content areas provide a rich and motivating context. Carefully crafted questions before, during, and after the reading enable students to develop and apply a strategic approach to comprehending text. Meaningful writing is also embedded throughout, as are level-appropriate suggestions for further reading to explore the topics. The *Annotated Teacher's Edition* includes background information for each selection, along with ideas for reteaching and extending key points.

Audience

Strategies for Reading is designed and paced to guide lower-achieving students to draw on what they already know, to read with questions in mind, to process the information given them, and to reach for meaning beyond the text—in short, to become strategic readers. The program is suitable for all students reading to obtain core knowledge in science and social studies.

Levels and Contents

There are four levels in the ***Strategies for Reading*** series.

Title	Curriculum Match/Interest Level	Readability Range
Avenues	Grade 3 up	2–3
Bridges	Grade 4 up	3–4
Crossroads	Grade 5 up	3–4
Directions	Grade 6 up	4–5

The contents of each ***Strategies for Reading*** book are organized around themes that relate to the content area curriculum framework of the main targeted grade. The social studies tie-ins are explicit: *Avenues* focuses on communities, *Bridges* highlights several key regions of the United States, *Crossroads* deals with U.S. history before the Civil War, and *Directions* encompasses the ancient world. The science connections evolve from the social studies themes, as appropriate to the level. Topics range across the life sciences, the earth sciences, the physical sciences, and technological applications. Here is an overview of the selection titles in each book:

AVENUES
(For grade 3 and up, readability 2–3)

UNIT ONE: COMMUNITIES BY THE SEA

Gifts from the Sea
Land's End
The Way It Used To Be
Hurricane!

UNIT TWO: LIVING IN CITIES

How Does a City Grow?
Wildlife in the City
A City's Bones
Plugging into Power

UNIT THREE: FARM AND RANCH LIFE

Bird Heroes
The Story of Dirt
Cow Town
Good Bugs, Bad Bugs

UNIT FOUR: DESERT COMMUNITIES

Anasazi: Ancient People of the Desert
Using Water
Santa Fe: Old Town, New Town
This, Too, Is Desert

BRIDGES
(For grade 4 and up, readability 3–4)

UNIT ONE: HIGHWAYS OF WATER

Father of Chicago
Can a Lake Die?
Mississippi Mound-Builders
Learning from the Past

UNIT TWO: WESTWARD HO!

The Western Story in Paint
Oh, Give Me a Home
The Mother of Texas
Folk Cures

UNIT THREE: GOLD!

Gold Fever
Mining for Gold
Giants
Mountain Man

UNIT FOUR: THE NEW LAND

Making Your Way in America
Lady Liberty
Famine!
A City's Roots

CROSSROADS
(For grade 5 and up, readability 3–4)

UNIT ONE: THE AGE OF DISCOVERY

Perils of the Sea
The Instruments of Discovery
The Journey of Cabeza de Vaca
To the Sea in Ships

UNIT TWO: COLONIAL AMERICA

A Threat of War
The Disease That Changed America
Ben Franklin's Secret
Electricity from the Sky

UNIT THREE: THE REVOLUTIONARY WAR

Nathan Hale: The Unlikely Spy
The Underwater Revolution
Deborah Sampson Goes to War
Banneker Looks to the Stars

UNIT FOUR: MOVING WEST

Pioneer Penney
Lewis and Clark Blaze a Trail
The Explorer-Scientists
The Night the Mississippi River Ran Backward

DIRECTIONS
(For grade 6 and up, readability 4–5)

UNIT ONE: ANCIENT EGYPT

A Queen Among Kings
Mummy
Fall of a Dynasty
Father Nile

UNIT TWO: THE GREEKS AND HEBREWS

Glory at Olympia
The Man Who Measured the Earth
Enemy at the Gates
Digging Up History

UNIT THREE: INDIA AND CHINA LONG AGO

Asoka Changes His Ways
When Is Zero Greater Than Nothing?
Building the Great Wall
South-Pointing Spoons and Exploding Powder

UNIT FOUR: THE ROMAN WORLD

The Day Pompeii Disappeared
Volcano
The Emperor and the Cross
The Technology of Empire

Structure

At each level, the *Strategies for Reading* books present four thematic units. Within each unit, two selections are directed toward scientific aspects of the theme and two feature elements from the social studies. Each unit is also designed around a consistent pattern for ease of student use. The subsections are:

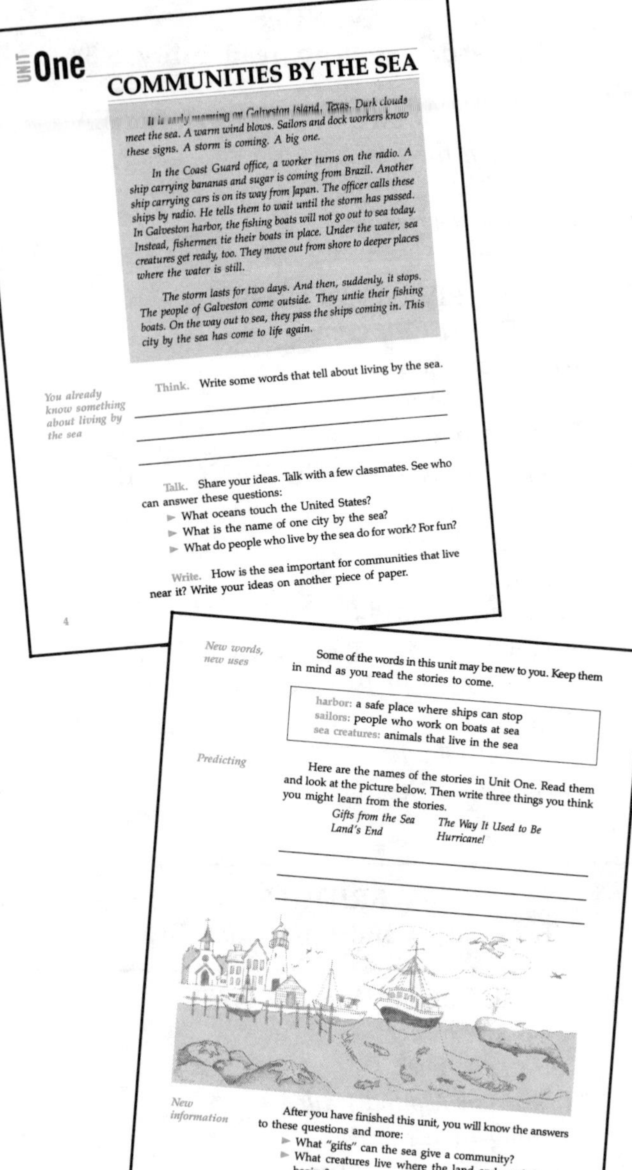

UNIT One

COMMUNITIES BY THE SEA

It is early morning on Galveston Island, Texas. Dark clouds meet the sea. A warm wind blows. Sailors and dock workers know these signs. A storm is coming. A big one.

In the Coast Guard office, a worker turns on the radio. A ship carrying bananas and sugar is coming from Brazil. Another ship carrying cars is on its way from Japan. The officer calls these ships by radio. He tells them to wait until the storm has passed. In Galveston harbor, the fishing boats will not go out to sea today. Instead, fishermen tie their boats in place. Under the water, sea creatures get ready, too. They move out from shore to deeper places where the water is still.

The storm lasts for two days. And then, suddenly, it stops. The people of Galveston come outside. They untie their fishing boats. On the way out to sea, they pass the ships coming in. This city by the sea has come to life again.

You already know something about living by the sea

Think. Write some words that tell about living by the sea.

Talk. Share your ideas. Talk with a few classmates. See who can answer these questions:

- What oceans touch the United States?
- What is the name of one city by the sea?
- What do people who live by the sea do for work? For fun?

Write. How is the sea important for communities that live near it? Write your ideas on another piece of paper.

4

New words, new uses

Some of the words in this unit may be new to you. Keep them in mind as you read the stories to come.

harbor: a safe place where ships can stop
sailors: people who work on boats at sea
sea creatures: animals that live in the sea

Predicting

Here are the names of the stories in Unit One. Read them and look at the picture below. Then write three things you think you might learn from the stories.

Gifts from the Sea *The Way It Used to Be*
Land's End *Hurricane!*

New information

After you have finished this unit, you will know the answers to these questions and more:

- What "gifts" can the sea give a community?
- What creatures live where the land ends and the sea begins?
- How did people use the sea long ago?
- What is a hurricane?

5

UNIT INTRODUCTION

- An *Overview Narrative* introduces the unit theme. Related in a general way to the four selections that follow, this brief passage serves as a springboard for tapping into students' prior knowledge. It also presents content-area vocabulary that will be used throughout the unit and assists students in predicting the unit contents.
- *You already know something about . . .* is a section that asks students to *Think, Talk,* and *Write* about ideas related to the unit theme.
- *New words, new uses* is a short glossary of content-area or specialized vocabulary that students will need to understand as they read the unit selections.
- *Predicting* lists the titles of the four selections in the unit and refers students to one or more graphics. Based upon this information, they are asked to predict three things they might learn as they read.
- *New information* gets students to think more about what they will be reading by summarizing the main idea of each selection in question form.

SELECTION-SPECIFIC PREREADING

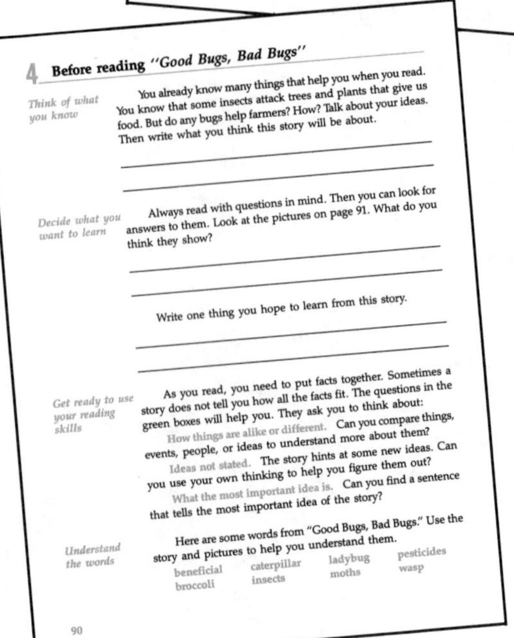

4 Before reading "Good Bugs, Bad Bugs"

Think of what you know

You already know many things that help you when you read. You know that some insects attack trees and plants that give us food. But do any bugs help farmers? How? Talk about your ideas. Then write what you think this story will be about.

Decide what you want to learn

Always read with questions in mind. Then you can look for answers to them. Look at the pictures on page 91. What do you think they show?

Write one thing you hope to learn from this story.

Get ready to use your reading skills

As you read, you need to put facts together. Sometimes a story does not tell you how all the facts fit. The questions in the green boxes will help you. They ask you to think about:

How things are alike or different. Can you compare things, events, people, or ideas to understand more about them?

Ideas not stated. The story hints at some new ideas. Can you use your own thinking to help you figure them out?

What the most important idea is. Can you find a sentence that tells the most important idea of the story?

Understand the words

Here are some words from "Good Bugs, Bad Bugs." Use the story and pictures to help you understand them.

beneficial broccoli caterpillar insects ladybug moths pesticides wasp

90

- *Think of what you know* offers two or three questions designed to guide students as they think about various aspects of a particular topic and recall any previous knowledge that they might bring to the reading.
- *Decide what you want to learn* helps students set the purpose for their reading.
- *Get ready to use your reading skills* alerts students to the types of reading strategies and critical thinking skills they might use to assist their comprehension of the passage.
- *Understand the words* lists potentially difficult vocabulary so that students can apply contex-

tual and visual clues to interpret them and teachers can preteach their meanings if it is appropriate.

NARRATIVE PASSAGE

- ☐ The three- to five-page ***Text*** focuses on a single aspect of the overall unit theme. Although simply written, each selection fully develops and explores the designated topic. Information-rich, the style is nonetheless riveting, almost magazinelike, to ensure student interest.
- ☐ ***Think About It*** questions in the margins highlight key information and help students process it effectively. They serve as a reminder that reading is an interactive activity—students must bring as much to the text as the text brings to them.
- ☐ ***Graphics***—in the form of illustrations, photographs, maps, charts, and graphs—appear on each page as an additional aid to comprehension.

SELECTION-SPECIFIC POSTREADING

- ☐ ***Think about the selection*** offers two to six open-ended questions, including one based on a graphic organizer, designed to help students confirm and extend what they have learned.
- ☐ ***Check what you learned*** is a self-monitoring feature that enables students to measure their progress toward the goals they set for themselves.
- ☐ ***Use your own words*** suggests a meaningful writing assignment to let students demonstrate their learning in their own words. Writing forms vary and include comparisons, descriptions, diary entries, letters, reports, essays, and so on.
- ☐ ***Find out more*** encourages students to pursue the topic further. It provides a brief bibliography of titles at an appropriate level that students can likely find in their school or local library.

UNIT REVIEW

- ☐ The last page of each unit combines multiple-choice and open-ended questions with an additional writing assignment. Its purpose is to help students perceive the connections among the selections they have read and to formulate their own conclusions about the topics presented under the theme umbrella.

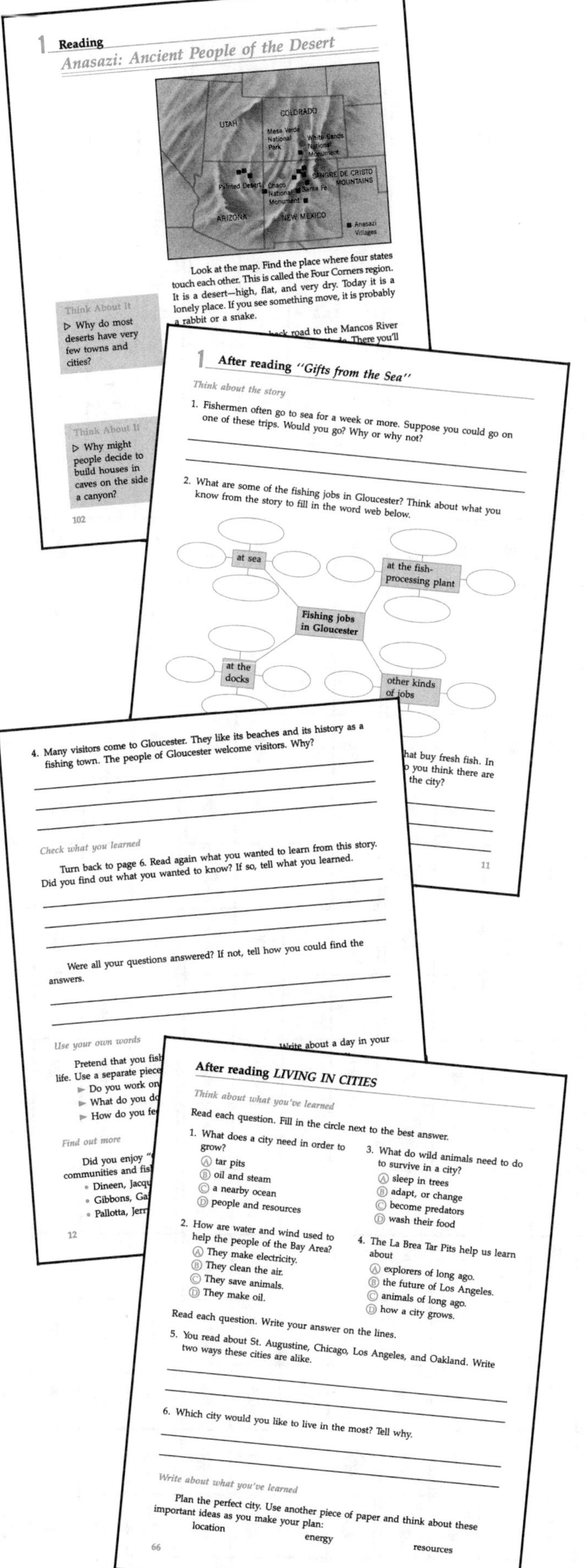

1 Reading
Anasazi: Ancient People of the Desert

Look at the map. Find the place where four states touch each other. This is called the Four Corners region. It is a desert—high, flat, and very dry. Today it is a lonely place. If you see something move, it is probably a rabbit or a snake.

Think About It
▷ Why do most deserts have very few towns and cities?

Think About It
▷ Why might people decide to build houses in caves on the side a canyon?

102

1 After reading "Gifts from the Sea"

Think about the story

1. Fishermen often go to sea for a week or more. Suppose you could go on one of these trips. Would you go? Why or why not?

2. What are some of the fishing jobs in Gloucester? Think about what you know from the story to fill in the word web below.

11

4. Many visitors come to Gloucester. They like its beaches and its history as a fishing town. The people of Gloucester welcome visitors. Why?

Check what you learned

Turn back to page 6. Read again what you wanted to learn from this story. Did you find out what you wanted to know? If so, tell what you learned.

Were all your questions answered? If not, tell how you could find the answers.

Use your own words

12

After reading LIVING IN CITIES

Think about what you've learned

Read each question. Fill in the circle next to the best answer.

1. What does a city need in order to grow?
   Ⓐ tar pits
   Ⓑ oil and steam
   Ⓒ a nearby ocean
   Ⓓ people and resources

2. How are water and wind used to help the people of the Bay Area?
   Ⓐ They make electricity.
   Ⓑ They clean the air.
   Ⓒ They save animals.
   Ⓓ They make oil.

3. What do wild animals need to do to survive in a city?
   Ⓐ sleep in trees
   Ⓑ adapt, or change
   Ⓒ become predators
   Ⓓ wash their food

4. The La Brea Tar Pits help us learn about
   Ⓐ explorers of long ago.
   Ⓑ the future of Los Angeles.
   Ⓒ animals of long ago.
   Ⓓ how a city grows.

Read each question. Write your answer on the lines.

5. You read about St. Augustine, Chicago, Los Angeles, and Oakland. Write two ways these cities are alike.

6. Which city would you like to live in the most? Tell why.

Write about what you've learned

Plan the perfect city. Use another piece of paper and think about these important ideas as you make your plan:
location energy resources

66

Strategies for Reading: Avenues

SCOPE & SEQUENCE

	UNIT ONE				UNIT TWO				UNIT THREE				UNIT FOUR			
	Gifts from the Sea	Land's End	The Way It Used to Be	Hurricane!	How Does a City Grow?	Wildlife in the City	A City's Bones	Plugging into Power	Bird Heroes	The Story of Dirt	Cow Town	Good Bugs, Bad Bugs	Anasazi: Ancient People of the Desert	Using Water	Santa Fe: Old Town, New Town	This, Too, Is Desert
Determining cause and effect	♦	♦	♦	♦	♦	♦	♦	♦	♦	♦	♦	♦	♦	♦	♦	♦
Recognizing points of view	♦		♦	♦	♦		♦		♦		♦				♦	
Comparing and contrasting	♦	♦			♦	♦		♦		♦		♦	♦	♦	♦	♦
Making predictions	♦	♦	♦	♦	♦	♦	♦	♦	♦	♦	♦	♦	♦	♦	♦	♦
Formulating inferences and conclusions	♦	♦	♦	♦	♦	♦	♦	♦	♦	♦	♦	♦	♦	♦	♦	♦
Establishing sequence		♦		♦	♦		♦	♦	♦			♦			♦	
Analyzing, evaluating, and synthesizing information	♦	♦	♦	♦	♦	♦	♦	♦	♦	♦	♦	♦	♦	♦	♦	♦
Identifying main ideas		♦										♦		♦		♦
Setting reading purpose	♦	♦	♦	♦	♦	♦	♦	♦	♦	♦	♦	♦	♦	♦	♦	♦
Expressing and supporting opinions	♦	♦	♦	♦	♦	♦	♦	♦	♦	♦	♦	♦	♦	♦	♦	♦
Interpreting visual aids	♦	♦	♦		♦	♦						♦				
Organizing information graphically	♦	♦	♦			♦		♦			♦	♦	♦		♦	♦
Inferring word meaning from context	♦	♦	♦	♦	♦	♦	♦	♦	♦	♦	♦	♦	♦	♦	♦	♦
Generating original ideas	♦	♦	♦	♦	♦	♦	♦	♦	♦	♦	♦	♦	♦	♦	♦	♦
Drawing on prior knowledge	♦	♦	♦	♦	♦	♦	♦	♦	♦	♦	♦	♦	♦	♦	♦	♦
Writing with purpose	♦	♦	♦	♦	♦	♦	♦	♦	♦	♦	♦	♦	♦	♦	♦	♦

Using *Strategies for Reading*

Strategies for Reading is designed to encourage students to interact positively with the text through the use of high-interest topics, gripping narrative style, abundant graphics, thought-provoking questions, and cooperative as well as independent learning approaches. In addition to a program overview (pages T4–T8), the *Annotated Teacher's Edition* offers overall suggestions for implementing the program (T9–T10) and background information for each of the units (T11–T16). This is followed by an exact replica of the student book, annotated with on-page suggestions for reinforcing and extending the learning.

Program Implementation

With its cross-curricular focus, ***Strategies for Reading*** can fit into your instructional plans in any number of ways. How you choose to use the program, along with the ability level of your students, will determine which of the suggestions provided in this section best meet your needs. The list is by no means exhaustive, and you will want to supplement it with your own store of methods and materials.

ORGANIZING RESOURCES

Before presenting each unit, you are encouraged to read the background information for it, as well as the suggestions for introducing and extending the specific theme. Previewing the student book selections is also recommended, since this will give you a general sense of the intent and structure of the unit. In addition, you may find it useful to:

- ☐ **Alert your school librarian** about the content the students are going to study. Potential titles for further reading are suggested at the end of the postreading section for each selection. Your librarian may be able to locate these or related works to encourage students to explore the topic on their own. If feasible, display the books in your classroom to attract student attention and promote interest.
- ☐ **Have available appropriate reference materials,** such as an atlas, an almanac, a globe, a dictionary, and a thesaurus. As students pose questions, suggest that they refer to these materials to see if they can discover the answers.

INCORPORATING DIRECTED AND COOPERATIVE LEARNING

Direct instruction remains the most effective means of enhancing student learning. Students can work through a great deal of ***Strategies for Reading*** on their own, but as appropriate or necessary, you may want to:

- ☐ **Model the processes.** If class discussion indicates students are having difficulty with a particular question or concept, think it through "out loud" with them. Show them how *you* would identify the relevant facts in the text, for example, and relate them to information you already know.
- ☐ **Use graphic organizers** to clarify points. Help students draw a flowchart, make an outline, sketch the scene, brainstorm a concept map—whatever is likely to give them a visual perspective on the issue(s).
- ☐ **Employ the QAR (question-answer relationships) technique.** Use inductive question-and-answer prompts to guide students as needed, but emphasize their own ability to problem-solve.

Strategies for Reading incorporates many opportunities for cooperative learning. Students are encouraged to discuss their ideas with classmates as well as to share their writing. The following suggestions will augment this process:

- ☐ **Form groups** using a system of random selection, such as birth months or counting-off in fours or fives, that will also ensure a broad spectrum of ability levels. Let each group select a leader, a recorder, and a checker.
- ☐ **Allow ample classtime** for assigned prereading discussions, for reviewing and discussing the during and after reading questions, and for actively debating points that interest students.
- ☐ **Make additional cooperative assignments.** Research projects, for example, might be excellent vehicles for pairs or groups to pool resources.
- ☐ **Encourage reciprocal teaching.** As students work with you and with each other, prompt the weaker learner to take over the teaching role from time to time. Research indicates that when students model teaching, they learn more.

DEVELOPING VOCABULARY

Understanding word meanings is a key component of reading comprehension, most especially in the comprehension of expository text. Potentially difficult or specialized vocabulary is listed in the prereading section so that students become aware of their presence. Usually the *Annotated Teacher's Edition* offers suggestions for developing an understanding of their meanings, but you may also want to keep in mind these general strategies:

- ☐ Have students **brainstorm** a group of related words to help them discover the meaning of the unknown one. Organize these into a **word web,** or **semantic map,** on the chalkboard or on chart paper. Here is an example:

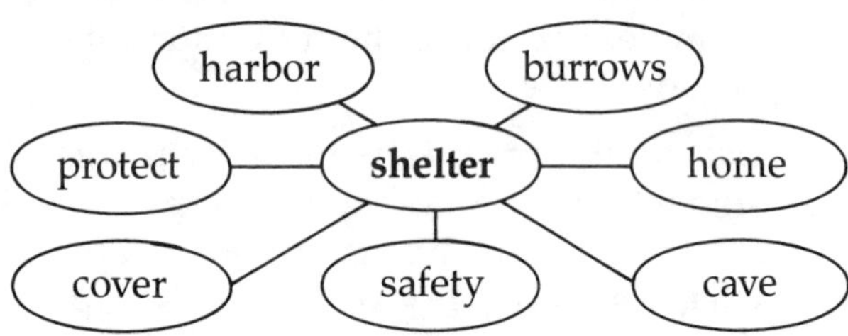

- ☐ Prepare **cloze** sentences or a cloze passage that provides additional context for inferring the meaning of the word. Here is an example:

  Animals that have been on the earth for a long time have had to change and learn new ways of living. They have _____ in order to survive.
  (*adapted*)

- ☐ Encourage a variety of **decoding** techniques. Guide students in identifying the root word (minus any affixes or inflectional endings), sounding out the syllables, and so on.
- ☐ Prepare **scripts** in which the dialogue features the unfamiliar words. Let groups of two to four characters memorize the parts and present the "skit" to the class. Then have everyone participate in interpreting the new words in the light of this new context.
- ☐ Refer students to the **dictionary** or a **thesaurus.** Have them look up the unfamiliar words and **write original sentences** using them to demonstrate their understanding of the definition(s) given.

ENHANCING MAP SKILLS

Many of the selections in ***Strategies for Reading*** are accompanied by a map to help students visualize the relevant locations. Questions pertaining directly to the maps focus on text comprehension and extension, but the maps can be used equally well to foster map-reading skills and an understanding of geography concepts. As students work with the maps, draw their attention to features shown (rivers, mountain ranges, etc.) and ask them interpretive questions involving cardinal and intermediate directions, the map key or legend, the scale of distance, the grid of coordinates, etc., as appropriate to the map.

INTEGRATING THE WRITING PROCESS

In the Unit Introduction, the postreading section for each selection, and the Unit Review, ***Strategies for Reading*** offers many and varied opportunities for students to engage in the writing process. This is basically a four-step procedure, with movement back and forth among the steps often creating a set of "substeps."

- ☐ **Prewriting:** Students decide what they want to say, how they will organize it, what form they will choose to express their ideas, and what audience they are writing for.
- ☐ **Writing:** Students make a quick draft of everything they wish to say about the topic, exercising maximum creativity without regard to the finer points of mechanics and usage.
- ☐ **Revising:** Students critique their work, conferencing with you or their peers. They correct their structure and organization and proofread for spelling, capitalization, punctuation, and usage.
- ☐ **Publishing:** Students share their written work with others. This may take the form of a presentation to the class, a display on the bulletin board, a final copy transcribed into their writing journal, etc.

The main goal of these writing assignments is to teach students to read, think, and write critically about a given topic. When you evaluate their work, tell students what you will be looking for. A holistic approach to the assessment may be most appropriate. Work with a fellow teacher to choose the criteria you will use and then assign an overall ranking from zero to four based on the *whole* work, rather than on specifics. Be sure to discuss each student's writing on an individual basis, explaining the reasons for your ranking and offering concrete suggestions for improvement.

Background Information

UNIT ONE: COMMUNITIES BY THE SEA
(Student book pages 4–35)

Historical Background

From earliest times, people have established settlements where the land meets the sea. They have learned to harvest the wealth of the sea and to navigate on its surface and beneath its waves. From hugging the coastline, early sailors gradually ventured farther and farther out until the seas were crossed and new settlements established on other coastlines. Always, however, those who live and work by the sea never forget its awesome power and therefore treat it with great respect.

The reading selections in Unit One describe the effects of the sea on both people and nature. The first selection, "Gifts from the Sea," gives an account of the fishing industry in Gloucester, Massachusetts. Gloucester has been an important seaport since it was first settled by the English in 1623. By 1700 the population had grown to 650. Lumber was plentiful, and shipbuilding and shipping became Gloucester's most important industries. To meet the large demand for American goods in the mid 1700s, Gloucester's fleet grew to forty boats. This fleet traveled to other American cities and all over the world. In the 1800s Gloucester became an important fishing center. A sudden abundance of mackerel in the 1820s led to a boom period in the fishing industry that lasted until 1900. From 1950 to the present, tourism, fishing, and fish-processing have been the city's three main industries. In the last few decades, however, fishermen and the fish-processing plants have been hurt by a diminishing supply of fish due to overfishing.

"Land's End" is the second selection in Unit One. It examines a different kind of coastal community—that of an ocean tide pool. Tide pools are found on rocky shores. They are natural basins in the rock that remain filled with sea water when the tide goes out. Most of these pools have permanent inhabitants, along with transients that may be washed in or out by the tides. The tides are caused mainly by the moon's gravitational pull. In most but not all coastal areas, the tides rise and fall twice in a period that is about 24 hours and 50 minutes long—the time between two rising moons. The area on a beach between the high tide line and the low tide line is called the tidal zone. It is here that shore life is most abundant during low tide. Besides the creatures that live in tide pools, there are insects, crustaceans, and mollusks buried in the sand or hidden in rocky clefts. Sea birds and mammals forage the strip for food.

"The Way It Used to Be" is the third selection. It takes readers back in time to the whaling days of the nineteenth century, when New Bedford, Massachusetts, was the whaling "capital" of the world. The whaling industry was very lucrative in New Bedford in the 1840s and 1850s. After building and outfitting a ship and paying the crew's salaries, an owner could expect to earn as much as $40,000 or more from a successful voyage. Whalemen were on board ship for months, even years, at a time. The captains would not allow their crews to gamble or be idle. When they weren't mending sails and "trying out" (rendering) the whale blubber, the crews often spent their free time carving scrimshaw—intricately designed tools and objects—out of baleen (whalebone). Contests were held every year in New Bedford for the best scrimshaw made by a whaleman. The cash prizes were as high as $500, and the captains usually won. The people of New Bedford were so thrifty that although the docks were lined with barrels of whale oil, the town stayed dark at night. The townspeople wanted the whale oil to sell, not to read by. The whaling industry began to decline as more and more people began using petroleum for lighting and heating their homes.

The scourge of coastal communities is the subject of the unit's final selection, "Hurricane!" The earliest written observations of hurricanes were recorded during the voyages of Christopher Columbus. Having learned about them on his first three voyages, Columbus was able to recognize an approaching hurricane on his fourth voyage. Before Columbus, the native peoples of the Caribbean knew very well about the fury of hurricanes. Some natives were reported to believe that hurricanes came from the gods, most notably from the evil god *Juracán*. People in other cultures call hurricanes by various names: In the Pacific Ocean, they are *typhoons;* in the Indian Ocean, *cyclones.* Filipinos call them *bahuios,* and Australians call them *willy-willies.* In any culture, however, moving away from the coast to higher ground remains the best protection against hurricanes. Even so, some hurricanes move quite far inland. In 1954, for instance, Hurricane Hazel devastated Toronto, Canada. The most severe hurricanes form in the Atlantic Ocean.

Introducing the Unit

Tell students that in this unit they will read about communities—human, animal, and plant—that exist in or near the sea. To begin, discuss the word *community.* Ask students to tell what a community is (an interacting population of various kinds of individuals in a common location) and to name some of its features. As students name features of a community, write their ideas on the chalkboard. Then ask the class to think about a community of sea creatures. How might it function?

Previewing the Reading Selections

Tell students to flip through the unit, noting the title of each reading selection and examining the graphics. Point out the different features of each lesson, focusing on the prereading section. Discuss with students different reading and thinking strategies (identifying main idea, empathizing, comparing, predicting, recognizing cause and effect, inferring, making judgments, etc.) they might find useful as they read each selection.

Extending the Unit

After students have completed their reading, have them work cooperatively, in small groups or in pairs, on a research project relating to some aspect of coastal communities. Here are some project ideas you may want to suggest:

- Write and illustrate a travel brochure extolling the scenery, history, leisure activities, etc., of a coastal community
- Create a booklet on hurricane preparedness, telling people what safety measures to take in the event of a disastrous storm
- Research and report on efforts to protect whales from extinction
- As a team of marine biologists, present an oral report, with illustrations, about the various types of whales, including where they are found and what their habits are
- Write a set of questions for an interview with a member of a tide pool community, focusing on the survival techniques it uses
- Create a set of qualifications and guidelines for hiring crew members for a deep sea commercial fishing venture

UNIT TWO: LIVING IN CITIES

(Student book pages 36–66)

Historical Background

Cities are organized communities that are home to thousands—often millions—of people. For about 5,500 years, cities have provided people with places to live, work, and gather together for purposes of entertainment (cultural and recreational), religious observance, and political decision-making. The selections in Unit Two present diverse aspects of life in a city, including growth, wildlife, paleontology, and infrastructure.

"How Does a City Grow?" is the unit's first selection. In it students will read about the contrasting growth patterns of two U.S. cities: St. Augustine, Florida, and Chicago, Illinois. With a current population of about 20,000, St. Augustine is the oldest city in the U.S. Spain first claimed Florida in 1513 and later founded St. Augustine to control the area and protect valuable shipping lanes in the Caribbean. Florida then came under U.S. control in 1821. The French explorers Marquette and Jolliet first came to the Chicago Portage (the land bridge that connects the Chicago River and Lake Michigan with the Des Plaines River) in 1673. Many Native Americans already lived there. In the 1830s some 3,000 Native Americans were forced by the U.S. government to leave the area; thousands of settlers soon occupied those lands. In 1837 Chicago became a city. The Great Chicago Fire of 1871 destroyed thousands of buildings. New ones were constructed of stone and steel, and Chicago later became famous as the birthplace of the skyscraper.

Unit Two's second selection, "Wildlife in the City," describes the adaptability of certain species of animals to an urban environment. Raccoons and opossums are among the wild animals that have adapted most successfully to urban life (others include squirrels, skunks, owls, foxes, and mice). Raccoons may live on the ground or in trees, alone or in family groups. Among their favorite foods are frogs, fish, eggs, fruit, nuts and seeds, and rodents. Scientists believe that dunking their food in water is an instinct remaining from a time when raccoons pulled much of their food from lakes and streams. Opossums are the only marsupials native to North America. The female carries her young in a pouch on her abdomen. When endangered, opossums will lie still and appear to be dead, thus giving rise to the expression "playing 'possum."

The third selection in Unit Two is "A City's Bones." It describes Los Angeles's prehistoric roots through the discovery of the La Brea fossils. More than one million individual fossils have been extracted from the La Brea Tar Pits, and many more remain. Discoveries include the bones of large animals, such as the saber-toothed cat and the imperial mammoth; the largest collection of bird fossils in the world (over 100,000 specimens); and fossilized plant materials, such as seeds, cones, leaves, and pollen. Together, these fossils have helped scientists construct a detailed picture of the life and climate of this region during the Ice Age. At the Page Museum, visitors can see tar pits as they looked years ago. They also can see workers removing, sorting, and cleaning fossils recently recovered.

"Plugging into Power," the unit's final selection, discusses urban infrastructure and technology, focusing on electricity. Light and heat are two important products of electricity, which also provides the power for many household appliances and industrial machines. Although many sources of electricity are currently in use, research continues to seek other less-expensive, renewable sources for the future. In 1988, almost 43 percent of California's electricity was generated by natural gas. Close to 19 percent came from hydroelectric power, with six percent coming from petroleum. The remaining 32 percent came from a variety of other sources, including more than 24 percent from nuclear power plants. In the San Francisco Bay Area, wind and geothermal power provide a higher percentage of energy than in other parts of the state.

Introducing the Unit

Begin by writing the population of your community on the chalkboard. Ask students if they know what that figure represents. Then ask if they think they live in a city. (Generally, a population of 2,500 or more is considered to be a city.) Lead students to recognize that a city is one kind of community; that is, a city is a community, but a community is not necessarily a city. Ask them to suggest as many features of a city as they can. To reinforce understanding of what makes a city, show the class photographs of communities from urban to rural and have students identify which ones are pictures of cities.

Previewing the Reading Selections

Tell students to flip through the unit, noting the title of each reading selection and examining the graphics. Point out the different features of each lesson, focusing on the prereading section. Discuss with students different reading and thinking strategies (identifying main idea, empathizing, comparing, predicting, recognizing cause and effect, inferring, making judgments, etc.) they might find useful as they read each selection.

Extending the Unit

After students have completed their reading, have them work cooperatively, in small groups or in pairs, on a research project relating to some aspect of urban life. Here are some project ideas you may want to suggest:

- Write a letter to several municipal chambers of commerce for information on industry, leisure and recreational activities, cultural amenities, etc., in their cities
- Prepare the script for an interview with a paleontologist about a recent discovery
- Create and perform a folk song about wild animals living in a city
- Write, illustrate, and present orally a myth to explain the origin and growth of your community
- Research and report on the infrastructure of your community: transportation systems, energy production, waste removal, and other city services

UNIT THREE: FARM AND RANCH LIFE
(Student book pages 67–98)

Historical Background

The practice of agriculture and animal husbandry began about 10,000 years ago when hunter-gatherers found that plants could be grown from seed and certain animals could be tamed. With the domestication of plants and animals, people no longer had to lead a nomadic existence. They could form communities. Through trial and error, early farmers and ranchers discovered selective breeding in order to raise stronger, more productive plants and animals. Gradually there were surpluses, so that a division of labor ensued: Some people stayed on the land to produce food; others moved to new communities where they developed other skills.

The selections in Unit Three explore land usage by people and animals, ways of getting products to market, and the exploitation of natural enmities to produce healthy crops. The first selection is "Bird Heroes," an account of the gulls that saved the Mormons' first Utah wheat crop from a swarm of crickets. In 1830 Joseph Smith founded the Church of Jesus Christ of Latter Day Saints at Fayette, New York, after having a vision of a prophet named Mormon. The Mormons soon moved to Ohio, then to Missouri and Illinois, where Smith was killed in 1844. Many of the Mormons, under the leadership of Brigham Young, moved farther west and founded Salt Lake City in 1847. It soon became an important trade center and stop on the westward trails. In 1896 Utah became a state, with Salt Lake City as its capital. At the city's heart is the Mormon

Tabernacle, and nearby is the monument to the gulls, designed by noted sculptor Mahonri Macintosh Young, a grandson of Brigham Young. The Great Salt Lake, a few miles away, is the nation's largest salt lake. It has an average depth of just 13 feet, and is saltier than the ocean.

The second selection in Unit Three is "The Story of Dirt." The two main ingredients of soil are rock particles and humus. Humus is organic material (dead plants and animals that have been partially decomposed by bacteria) that furnishes nutrients to plants, allowing them to grow. The three types of rock particles—sand, silt, and clay—have distinct properties. Clay is the smallest particle and holds water the best. Sand, the largest, allows water to drain through better than clay or silt. Thus, a combination of the three, known as loam, provides the best soil for cultivation. One of the most important soil management techniques used by farmers is crop rotation, the planting of different crops in one field at different times. This technique includes allowing fields to "rest," or lie fallow. Farmers also add fertilizer to soil to enrich it.

"Cow Town" is the unit's third selection. Abilene, Kansas, became the first cow town in 1867, but it was soon followed by others. Cattle were plentiful in Texas after the Civil War, and many newly freed African Americans went there to work as cowboys. Beef was in great demand in eastern cities, so cattle trails were established to move the great herds. The route from Texas to Kansas was relatively unpopulated, allowing cattle to be driven overland to the new railheads of Kansas. The era was short-lived, though: Cattle lost too much weight on the long drive, farmers began to fence the land, new railheads were opened up, and harsh weather devastated many herds. By the mid-1880s, the heyday of the cow towns and the long drive was over. Cowboys continued to work on ranches, however, and this remained an attractive alternative for African Americans, who enjoyed relative freedom from discrimination in this occupation.

In the final selection, "Good Bugs, Bad Bugs," the practice of using beneficial insects to control insects that attack crops is traced to 324 B.C. Chinese farmers began then to use ants to attack caterpillars and beetles that destroyed their citrus trees. These farmers went so far as to build bridges between the trees to make it easier for the ants to do their job. China is considered the world leader in the use of beneficial insects to protect crops, using such techniques on more than 21 million acres. Widespread concern about the harmful side effects of pesticides has led to increased interest in such "biological pest controls" in this country. A number of companies now market beneficial insects to farmers and gardeners across the country.

Introducing the Unit

Ask students if they know where food products that are part of their daily lives come from. For example, dairy products, including milk, cream, butter, cheese, cottage cheese, yogurt, and ice cream, come from cows on dairy farms; beef comes from cattle raised on cattle ranches; vegetables come from farms; cereal, bread, and pasta come from farm-grown grains such as wheat, corn, oats, rice, rye, and barley; etc. You might use a flow chart to show how products grown or raised on a farm or ranch wind up on people's tables. Then ask students to name a favorite meal, such as pizza or cheeseburger. Help them to name the component ingredients of the food and tell where each ingredient originated in order to emphasize the importance of farms and ranches in their lives.

Previewing the Reading Selections

Tell students to flip through the unit, noting the title of each reading selection and examining the graphics. Point out the different features of each lesson, focusing on the prereading section. Discuss with students different reading and thinking strategies (identifying main idea, empathizing, comparing, predicting, recognizing cause and effect, inferring, making judgments, etc.) they might find useful as they read each selection.

Extending the Unit

After students have completed their reading, have them work cooperatively, in small groups or in pairs, on a research project relating to some aspect of farm and ranch life. Here are some project ideas you may want to suggest:

- Create a mural or diorama to show farm and ranch life
- Write a script for a documentary on a day in the life of a farmer or rancher
- Research and report on a farm crop, tracing it from seed through processing and packaging
- Draw a diagram and explain the function of some type of machinery or equipment used in farming or ranching, such as a combine, grain elevator, automatic milking machine, thresher, harvester, etc.

- If facilities are available, plant and tend a small vegetable garden
- Report on farming and ranching in other parts of the world
- Write a biography of Charles "Turnip" Townshend, the man who invented the system of crop rotation

UNIT FOUR: DESERT COMMUNITIES

(Student book pages 99–128)

Historical Background

Including polar regions, deserts make up around one-sixth of the earth's surface, with warm deserts taking up most of that area. The desert belts that ring the earth lie between 15 and 35 degrees north and south of the equator. In these zones, mountains may block moisture-carrying winds, or atmospheric conditions may generally prevent rain from falling. Some desert regions, such as the Gobi in central Asia, are simply too far from oceans to feel the effects of rain-bearing clouds. The second largest desert in the world, after the Sahara, is the desert of central Australia. Though seemingly inhospitable to plant and animal life, deserts are home to many species of flora and fauna which have successfully adapted to a dry environment. Deserts are also rich in mineral deposits.

The reading selections in Unit Four describe human settlements in the desert, indigenous flora and fauna, and several vastly different desert regions. The first selection is "Anasazi: Ancient People of the Desert." The Four Corners is that area where the states of Colorado, New Mexico, Utah, and Arizona meet. It is a dry canyon and mesa region that contains the sites of many Anasazi settlements. Mesa Verde, in Colorado, is one of the most spectacular of these. It was declared a National Park in 1906. Other awe-inspiring ruins are found at Canyon de Chelly, Arizona, and Bandelier, New Mexico. The Anasazi are also known as the "cliff dwellers." Their descendants today are the Pueblo people, a group that includes the Hopi and Zuni. Many Pueblo people still live in stone or adobe community houses in the western Rio Grande valley, which runs north-south through central New Mexico.

In "Using Water," the second selection in Unit Four, students will become acquainted with two water-efficient denizens of the desert, the horned lizard and the saguaro cactus. There are thirteen species of horned lizards, seven of which are found in the United States. These creatures are sometimes called "horny toads" because of their rough skin and ability to inflate themselves with air, thus preventing predators from swallowing them. Their main food is ants, but they also eat other insects. The saguaro cactus, known as the "trademark of Arizona," is the largest cactus in the United States. It takes between 150 and 200 years to reach full size. Most of a saguaro's weight—up to 90 percent—comes from its stored water. The fruit of the saguaro has long been prized by Native Americans in the Southwest. The name *saguaro* comes from a Pima word meaning "friend." Today, saguaros are endangered by disease and human activity.

The third selection in Unit Four is "Santa Fe: Old Town, New Town." No one knows when the first people settled around Santa Fe, though the Anasazi were there at least 1,000 years ago. The Spanish explorer Coronado came in 1540, and the first Spanish colony was founded in 1548. Mexican independence from Spain in 1821 helped open the town to American trade and influence, and the Mexican War of 1846-1848 resulted in Santa Fe and most of the Southwest becoming part of the United States. The Santa Fe Trail, which stretched overland to Missouri, was the main route to Santa Fe until the railroad was completed in 1880. Today Santa Fe, with a population of about 50,000, is the capital of New Mexico. It is widely known for its thriving arts and crafts community and diverse culture.

The unit's final selection is "This, Too, Is Desert." The earth is home to widely different types of desert. If a major criterion for a desert region is ten inches or less of rainfall a year, then the frozen tundra of the Arctic and the icy, windswept, barren land of Antarctica certainly qualify. And yet, these regions, too, are home to flora and fauna that have successfully adapted to a harsh environment. While weather patterns that cause deserts have remained fairly constant for hundreds of years, growing populations requiring more land on which to raise crops have led to the expansion of many deserts. Desertification results from overgrazing of livestock, poor farming techniques, loss of trees, and mining. Steps are being taken to reverse this trend. New trees are being planted to keep sand from blowing onto crops, and new farming techniques are being used to keep the soil from wearing out.

Introducing the Unit

Ask students what they do when they are so hot and so thirsty that they don't think they can take it for another minute. When some of them answer that they go inside, explain that this is what people and animals in the desert do, too: they go inside a cave or building with thick walls, or they go underground. Then show students pictures of life in various deserts around the world. They might be interested to learn about the town of Coober Pedy in the Australian Desert, which is built entirely underground. The area is rich in opals, but the ground surface is too hot for human habitation, so miners and their families have literally "gone underground."

Previewing the Reading Selections

Tell students to flip through the unit, noting the title of each reading selection and examining the graphics. Point out the different features of each lesson, focusing on the prereading section. Discuss with students different reading and thinking strategies (identifying main idea, empathizing, comparing, predicting, recognizing cause and effect, inferring, making judgments, etc.) they might find useful as they read each selection.

Extending the Unit

After students have completed their reading, have them work cooperatively, in small groups or in pairs, on a research project relating to some aspect of desert communities. Here are some project ideas you may want to suggest:

- Write and illustrate a travel brochure about the beauties of a particular desert region
- Research and report on prospecting for minerals in the desert
- Create a diorama to show the flora and fauna of a desert
- Draw a map of the world showing its desert regions with each desert's most important feature shown as a symbol
- Present an illustrated oral report on a plant or animal of the desert

STRATEGIES FOR READING

Avenues

by Lana Costantini

ISBN 0-8454-2533-1

CONTINENTAL PRESS
Elizabethtown, PA 17022

Educational Consultants

Dr. Katherine A. Kane
San Diego, CA

Dr. Betty Willis
Houston, TX

James P. Menconi
Chicago, IL

Dr. Helen W. Turner
Washington, DC

Al Salesky
New York City, NY

Cover Design

Kirchoff/Wohlberg, Inc.

Cover Photograph

Rafael Macia/Photo Researchers, Inc.

Interior Design

Pat Gavett

Illustrations

Ray Burns, pages 23, 24, 39, 63, 71, 72
Margaret Sanfilippo, pages 5, 8, 9, 10, 46, 48, 85, 104, 117
V. Carlin Verreaux, pages 15, 16, 17, 30, 31, 54, 56, 61, 68, 77, 79, 80, 91, 92, 94, 100, 110, 118

Cartography

Masami Miyamoto

Photo Credits

Page 7, AP/Wide World Photos; 14A, 14B, Animals Animals/Zig Leszczynski; 22, The Granger Collection; 25, Animals Animals/James D. Watt; 29, 32, 40, AP/Wide World Photos; 42, © Hap Stewart/Jeroboam, Inc.; 47, Animals Animals/Michael Leach; 53, © Bill Aron/Jeroboam, Inc.; 55, Courtesy of the George C. Page Museum; 60, © Roy Shigley/Jeroboam, Inc.; 62, © Olof Kallstrom/Jeroboam, Inc.; 73, The Salt Lake Convention & Visitors Bureau; 78, Animals Animals/Stouffer Prod. Ltd.; 84, The Granger Collection; 93, AP/Wide World Photos; 103, Mesa Verde National Park; 105, Art Hutchinson; 109, Animals Animals/Breck P. Kent; 111, Earth Scenes/Leonard Lee Rue III; 115, Mark Nohl, New Mexico Economic & Tourism Dept.; 116, © Dave Glaubinger/Jeroboam, Inc.; 122, Earth Scenes/Doug Allan; 124, Animals Animals/Leonard Lee Rue III; 125, Earth Scenes/R. Ingo Riepl

Teacher Material

Straight Line Editorial Development, Inc.: Larry DiStasi, Marjorie Glazer, Brent Goff, Peder Jones, Noel Kaufman, Mariah Marvin, Michael Miovic, Rob Moore, Penn Mullin, Lorraine Sintetos, Sally Wittman, Lisa Yount

CONTENTS

UNIT One

COMMUNITIES BY THE SEA

To start:
Galveston, on Galveston Island about two miles off the coast of Texas, is a vital seaport on the Gulf of Mexico. Exports include cotton, rice, and oil-drilling equipment; imports include automobiles, bananas, tea, and sugar. In 1900 a hurricane killed more than 6,000 people. Since then, a seventeen-foot-high seawall has been built for protection. Sophisticated weather-tracking equipment also warns citizens of impending storms. Ask students why they think ships are told not to enter the harbor and why sea creatures move farther out to sea when a storm is brewing.

It is early morning on Galveston Island, Texas. Dark clouds meet the sea. A warm wind blows. Sailors and dock workers know these signs. A storm is coming. A big one.

In the Coast Guard office, a worker turns on the radio. A ship carrying bananas and sugar is coming from Brazil. Another ship carrying cars is on its way from Japan. The officer calls these ships by radio. He tells them to wait until the storm has passed. In Galveston harbor, the fishing boats will not go out to sea today. Instead, fishermen tie their boats in place. Under the water, sea creatures get ready, too. They move out from shore to deeper places where the water is still.

The storm lasts for two days. And then, suddenly, it stops. The people of Galveston come outside. They untie their fishing boats. On the way out to sea, they pass the ships coming in. This city by the sea has come to life again.

You already know something about living by the sea

Think. Write some words that tell about living by the sea.

Students' responses will vary. Possibilities include: boats, ships, beaches, fish, nets, seagulls, sailing. Encourage students to discuss and explain their answers.

Students might name the Pacific, Atlantic, and Arctic oceans; various coastal cities; and occupations ranging from fishing to oil drilling to shipping.

Talk. Share your ideas. Talk with a few classmates. See who can answer these questions:

- What oceans touch the United States?
- What is the name of one city by the sea?
- What do people who live by the sea do for work? For fun?

Write. How is the sea important for communities that live near it? Write your ideas on another piece of paper.

Have students share their writing. You might use some of their ideas as part of a bulletin board display on the importance of the sea in our lives.

New words, new uses

Some of the words in this unit may be new to you. Keep them in mind as you read the stories to come.

harbor: a safe place where ships can stop
sailors: people who work on boats at sea
sea creatures: animals that live in the sea

Predicting

Here are the names of the stories in Unit One. Read them and look at the picture below. Then write three things you think you might learn from the stories.

Gifts from the Sea *The Way It Used to Be*
Land's End *Hurricane!*

Students will learn about: (1) fishing in Gloucester, Massachusetts; (2) the creatures that inhabit an ocean tide pool; (3) nineteenth-century whaling out of New Bedford, Massachusetts; and (4) the effects of hurricanes on coastal communities and what can be done to mitigate these effects.

New information

Discuss the reasons for these questions. (They provide focus for the reading.) Explain that when reading for information, it is important to set purposes ahead of time.

After you have finished this unit, you will know the answers to these questions and more:

- What "gifts" can the sea give a community?
- What creatures live where the land ends and the sea begins?
- How did people use the sea long ago?
- What is a hurricane?

Call students' attention to the illustration on this page, and ask them what they see in it. Help them to recognize several of the components of a coastal community—human, animal, and plant.

1 Before reading *"Gifts from the Sea"*

Think of what you know

You already know many things that help you when you read. What jobs do people in your community have? Now think about a town near the sea. What work might people do there? Talk about your ideas. Then write what you think this story will be about.

This selection describes the fishing industry in Gloucester, Massachusetts. Readers follow the crew of a small trawler to discover the kinds of boats fishermen use, where they fish, what they catch, and the equipment and forecasting systems that make fishing today less dangerous than in the past. Shore activities that relate to the fishing industry and the pride of the Gloucester community in its fishermen are also included. Discuss with students the importance of the sea in the daily life of a fishing community. Also have them consider the dangers faced by people who catch fish for a living. Encourage students to share their predictions about the selection's content.

Decide what you want to learn

Always read with questions in mind. Then you can look for answers to them. Study the picture on page 10. Tell what you see.

A young girl watches the crew of a fishing boat as they prepare their catch for storage in the boat's hold.

Write one thing you hope to learn from this story.

Students may be interested to know what kinds of fish are caught or how they are processed.

Get ready to use your reading skills

As you read, you need to put facts together. Sometimes a story does not tell you how all the facts fit. The questions in the green boxes will help you. They ask you to think about:

Why people do things. Can you use what people say and do to figure out why they act the way they do?

Where the facts lead. You already know some facts. Others are given in the story. Can you put them together to figure out new ideas?

Understand the words

Here are some words from "Gifts from the Sea." Use the story and pictures to help you understand them.

cod	**flounder**	**statue**
crafts	**rot**	**trawler**
fish-processing	**shrimp**	**whiting**

To help students with new vocabulary, create a semantic map around the word *fishing* on the chalkboard. Discuss each new word as it relates to fishing. You might ask volunteers to look up the words *whiting* and *flounder* in a dictionary.

1 Reading

Gifts from the Sea

Think About It

▷ The fisherman in the statue is dressed for a storm and gripping the wheel of his boat. Why do you think the artist showed him like that?

Light from the moon shines on the dark ocean. A fishing boat drags its net under the water. Sea birds scream overhead. They wait for the fish to be pulled in. It is Maria's first time out at night with her father. She is too excited to sleep. Finally, the long hours of dragging the net are over. What surprises will she find in the net? Crabs? Brown seaweed 30 feet long?

Maria's dad, Franco, is excited, too. So are the other two men on the boat. But they aren't thinking about crabs or seaweed. They are thinking about fish. What kinds of fish will there be? How big? How many? Like 800 other men in Gloucester, they catch fish for a living.

Gloucester is an important fishing town in Massachusetts. It is north of Boston on the Atlantic coast. More than 200 fishing boats work out of its harbor. The fishermen of Gloucester catch more fish than any other fishermen in the state.

The sea has always been the center of life in Gloucester. The people of Gloucester have placed a statue of a fisherman in front of the harbor. He seems to watch over the boats that go to sea.

Possible responses to the question above include: The artist wanted to show how hard the life of a fisherman is and how brave fishermen are. You may want to model how students can draw this conclusion from information stated in the story along with what they already know.

You might point out that knowing the fishermen are hopeful about the success of their catch helps readers understand their excitement.

Most Gloucester fishermen use boats called **trawlers.** A trawler has a net called a *trawl.* The trawl is shaped like a bag. The trawler drags its trawl under water so that it fills with fish.

Possible responses to the first question below include: Small boats don't have enough fuel or power to go so far out to sea; they cannot carry nets large enough to make such a long trip worthwhile. You may want to ask students to compare and contrast small and large trawlers to help them arrive at their conclusions.

For the second question below, radios help fishermen by warning them about storms. Radios also allow fishermen to let people on shore know when a boat is in trouble. Stronger boats help fishermen out at sea to weather high seas during storms.

Franco's boat is a small trawler. It is about as long as a school bus. Small trawlers fish in the warmer waters near the shore. In the summer, these boats catch whiting. In the winter, they catch shrimp and sometimes cod.

Larger trawlers go to sea for a week to 10 days at a time. They can go farther from shore. The water is much colder out there. The large trawlers catch cod and other kinds of fish.

Many trawlers fish near the Gloucester shore. They also fish farther north. But only large trawlers fish in the open sea south and east of Gloucester. That is where the rich fishing grounds of George's Bank are found. George's Bank is more than 100 miles from land.

People have been fishing out of Gloucester for more than 350 years. During that time, many fishermen have been lost in storms at sea. But in the last 20 years, fewer fishermen have been lost. Boats are stronger. They also have a special radio that lets the fishermen talk to people on shore. Today people are better at knowing when a storm is on the way. Franco listened to a weather report before he and Maria left the dock.

Think About It

▷ Why don't small trawlers fish in George's Bank?

▷ How do you think radios and stronger boats help fishermen?

Possible response to the question in the first box: Throwing back into the sea fish that are too small helps those fish to grow into adults and breed. This increases the fish population so there will be enough to catch in the future.

Think About It

▷ Fishermen can't keep some kinds of fish if they are under a certain size. How might this help fishermen?

Fishing is safer today. But fishermen like Franco are having a problem making enough money. Over the years, too many people have fished in these waters. There are not as many fish as there used to be. About 20 years ago, there were two times as many of the fish Franco catches.

Fishing is hard in other ways for fishermen and their families. The fishermen must work as much as they can in the warm months of the year. In the winter, bad weather can keep them away from the sea for weeks. Maria likes the winter months, though. She gets to spend more time with her father.

In the summer, Franco goes out to sea almost every day. But once every two weeks he stays on shore. He and his men clean the boat and fix the fishing nets. They also pack food, gas, and ice for the next two weeks. Maria likes to help her father at the docks.

Think About It

▷ Fishermen are not home very much during the spring, summer, and fall. What do you think life is like for their families?

Sometimes Franco and his crew go out for many days at a time. They work almost all day and all night. They take turns sleeping when the net is dragged. Today, though, Maria and Franco have gone out on a short trip. They left the dock at 2:00 in the morning. They'll come back late in the afternoon.

For the question in the second box, help students conclude that their families probably miss fishermen when they are away. Those at home probably must learn to do a lot of things for themselves.

The hardest work on a fishing boat begins when the net is pulled in. This time, the net has about 10,000 whiting and flounder, and lots of brown seaweed! It is a good catch. Maria watches the men sort the fish. Then they cut each fish open and take out the insides. If they don't do this, the fish will rot. All the fish are then packed into the bottom of the boat and covered with ice.

The fishermen drag the ocean bottom once more. Finally, it is time to go back to shore. Franco brings the boat to a dock in front of a fish-processing plant. The plant workers take the fish inside. They wash and skin each one. They also cut each fish into pieces and take out the bones. Then they press the fish into large blocks and freeze them. Sometimes the blocks are cut into small pieces and coated with bread crumbs. Then they are sold.

For the question below, students may include fishermen, boat dock workers, fish-processing plant workers, fish market workers, restaurant workers, artists, and any other occupation they can logically justify.

Think About It

▷ How many different jobs does fishing give the people of Gloucester?

Many people in Gloucester make their living off of gifts from the sea. People work on boats and in fish-processing plants. They work on the docks and in fish markets. Restaurants serve food from the sea. Artists use things from the sea to make arts and crafts. Everywhere you go are signs of the sea.

1 After reading *"Gifts from the Sea"*

Think about the story

1. Fishermen often go to sea for a week or more. Suppose you could go on one of these trips. Would you go? Why or why not?

Answers will vary. Encourage students to give at least one reason to support their opinions and feelings.

2. What are some of the fishing jobs in Gloucester? Think about what you know from the story to fill in the word web below.

Answers will vary, but may include some of the following jobs:

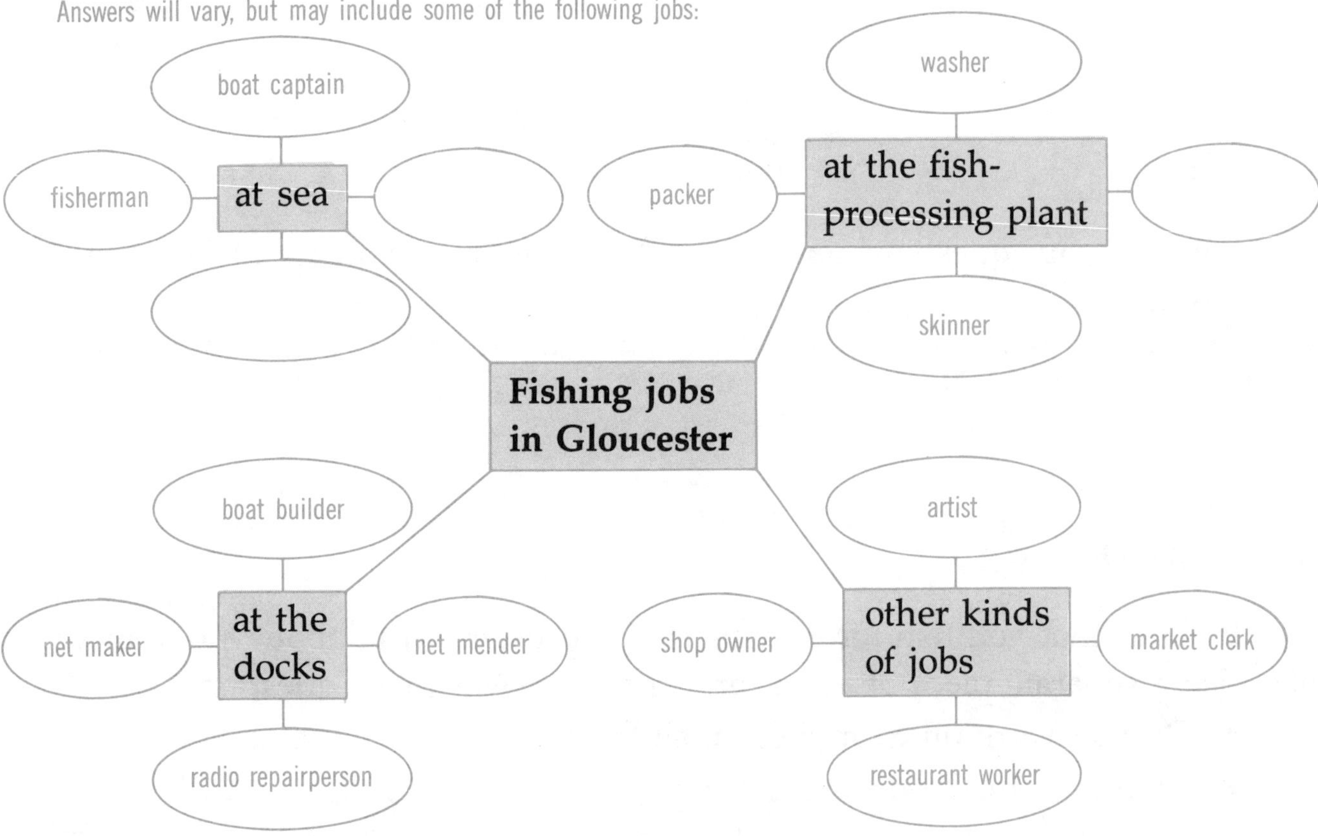

3. Gloucester now has only three fish-processing plants that buy fresh fish. In 1900, there were more than 100 of these plants. Why do you think there are so few these days? How do you think this has changed the city?

Answers will vary. Students may suggest that overfishing is the main reason for the decrease in the number of fish-processing plants, or they may note that modern plants are probably much larger than the older ones.

4. Many visitors come to Gloucester. They like its beaches and its history as a fishing town. The people of Gloucester welcome visitors. Why?

Answers will vary. Some students may focus on the pride of the people of Gloucester in their fishing history, while others may note that tourists are an important part of the city today. Help students understand that the money tourists spend on food, hotels, and souvenirs helps the economy of the entire community.

Check what you learned

Turn back to page 6. Read again what you wanted to learn from this story. Did you find out what you wanted to know? If so, tell what you learned.

Answers will vary depending on the goals students set for themselves.

Were all your questions answered? If not, tell how you could find the answers.

Students may mention going to the library as a way to find answers to their questions. In addition, call students' attention to the titles of the books suggested at the bottom of this page.

Use your own words

Pretend that you fish for a living in Gloucester. Write about a day in your life. Use a separate piece of paper and try to answer these questions:

- Do you work on a large or small trawler?
- What do you do during the day?
- How do you feel at the end of the day?

You may want students to follow the steps of the writing process described on page T10 of this Annotated Teacher's Edition to complete this activity. Invite students to take turns reading aloud their finished writing.

Find out more

Did you enjoy "Gifts from the Sea"? If so, read more about fishing communities and fishing. Look for these books in your library:

- Dineen, Jacqueline. *Food from the Sea.* Young Library, 1986.
- Gibbons, Gail. *Surrounded by Sea.* Little, Brown, 1991.
- Pallotta, Jerry. *Going Lobstering.* Charlesbridge, 1990.

2 Before reading *"Land's End"*

Think of what you know

You already know many things that help you when you read. Have you ever been to an ocean beach? Have you seen or read about animals that live on rocky ocean shores? Talk about your ideas. Then write what you think this story will be about.

This selection describes an ocean tide pool and the sea creatures that inhabit it. It relates how these animals protect themselves at low tide from too much sun and too little water and explains the important role of algae in maintaining tide pool life. Finally, it discusses high tide and how the food chain operates as the various creatures feed on each other in order to survive. Have students discuss their own experiences visiting a sea, lake, or river shore. Explain that in a community of plants and animals, each living thing depends on other living things for survival. Students may predict that the selection will be about watching the animals that live along the water's edge.

Decide what you want to learn

Always read with questions in mind. Then you can look for answers to them. Look at the pictures on pages 14 and 16. What do you think they show?

The photographs on page 14 show an ocean tide pool at low and high tide. The illustration on page 16 is a cross section of an ocean tide pool, showing the different levels occupied by various sea animals.

Write one thing you hope to learn from this story.

Students may be interested to learn about the lives of the sea creatures that inhabit an ocean tide pool.

Get ready to use your reading skills

As you read, you need to put facts together. Sometimes a story does not tell you how all the facts fit. The questions in the green boxes will help you. They ask you to think about:

What the most important idea is. Can you find a sentence that tells the most important idea of the story?

Why things happen. Can you figure out why something happens in the story? Can you see what happens because of it?

How things are alike or different. Can you compare things, events, people, or ideas to understand more about them?

Understand the words

Here are some words from "Land's End." Use the story and pictures to help you understand them.

algae	**mussels**	**sea anemone**
barnacles	**oxygen**	**slippery**
limpets	**plankton**	

To help students with new vocabulary, read each word aloud and have students repeat it. Ask them to create a chalkboard drawing of a rocky seashore. Add informational labels, using some of the new words.

2 Reading

Land's End

Answers for the question below will vary, but students may suggest that when the tide comes in, tide pool creatures are hidden from view by the water. Students may also point out that wave action or sunlight reflecting off the water might make it hard to see below the surface.

Think About It

▷ Why can't you always see creatures who live in a tide pool?

Walk along a rocky shore in late afternoon. Crying sea birds circle in the sky. You can see and hear nothing else in this quiet place. Yet millions of things live just a few steps away. Climb down the rocks toward the ocean. The rocks are sharp and slippery. Make your way carefully to the water's edge. What creatures have their homes here?

You cannot always see the creatures who live here. Two times a day the tide is high. Then the sea comes in and covers these rocks. Two times a day the tide goes out. Then the rocks are bare. But some water stays behind in deep holes in the rocks. These holes filled with sea water are called **tide pools.**

Now the tide is out. We can see the creatures who live in the tide pools and on the rocks around them. Look carefully. There are living things all around you.

Low tide

High tide

For the question below: These creatures will dry up without water, and since they cannot move down into the water when the tide ebbs, they must hold water in order to survive. You may want to model using facts from the selection (*Inside every shell is a soft creature that can't live if it dries up.*) along with prior knowledge (when the water level drops, things above it dry out) to answer this question.

Think About It

▷ Why do you think barnacles and mussels need to store sea water?

Shells of different sizes and colors cover the rocks at your feet. Those large, dark blue ones are called **mussels.** The tiny white cones are **barnacles,** and the brown cones are **limpets.** Inside every shell is a soft creature that can't live if it dries up. So each one took in some water before the tide went out. Then it closed up tight.

All these animals are held fast to the rock. Not even a great wave can pull them off. Mussels and barnacles make their own sticky glues. They stay in one spot all their lives. The limpet is a snail that moves when it eats. So it has a strong "foot" that helps it hold onto the rock.

Now, look down into the tide pool. The sides and bottom are covered with seaweed. It seems to come in every color and shape. These plants are called **algae.**

Think About It

▷ What might happen if you planted some algae in a garden with land plants? Why?

Algae get their food from water, just as land plants do. But algae are different from land plants. Algae don't drink through roots. Every part of algae takes in water. And, instead of roots, algae have a bottom part called a **holdfast.** The holdfast holds tightly onto the rock. That way, the plant will not be washed away.

The algae would not survive because they do not have roots to draw nutrients and water from the soil; they need to be covered with water to survive. Explain that knowing how algae get their food helps lead to the conclusion that they could not survive out of water.

Answers to the question below will vary. Possible responses include: There are many kinds of tide pool creatures; tide pool creatures can't live if they dry up; algae provide food, oxygen, and shelter

Think About It

▷ What are the most important ideas to remember about tide pool creatures?

for other tide pool creatures. If students have difficulty identifying the important ideas, discuss the difference between a main idea and a supporting detail.

Without algae, animals could not live in the pool. As the algae make their own food, they put oxygen into the water. Like people, sea animals must have oxygen to live. Along with giving oxygen, algae give the tide pool animals food and homes. The animals find good hiding places in the algae as well.

Near the pool's edge, a sea star hides in wet seaweed. Other animals, too, are hiding from the drying sun. A crab has crawled under a rock. Some animals on the walls have closed up into ugly bumps.

Only at the pool bottom do animals still move. Mud snails are still looking for things to eat. And tiny shrimp, snails, and crabs hunt for worms in a forest of seaweed.

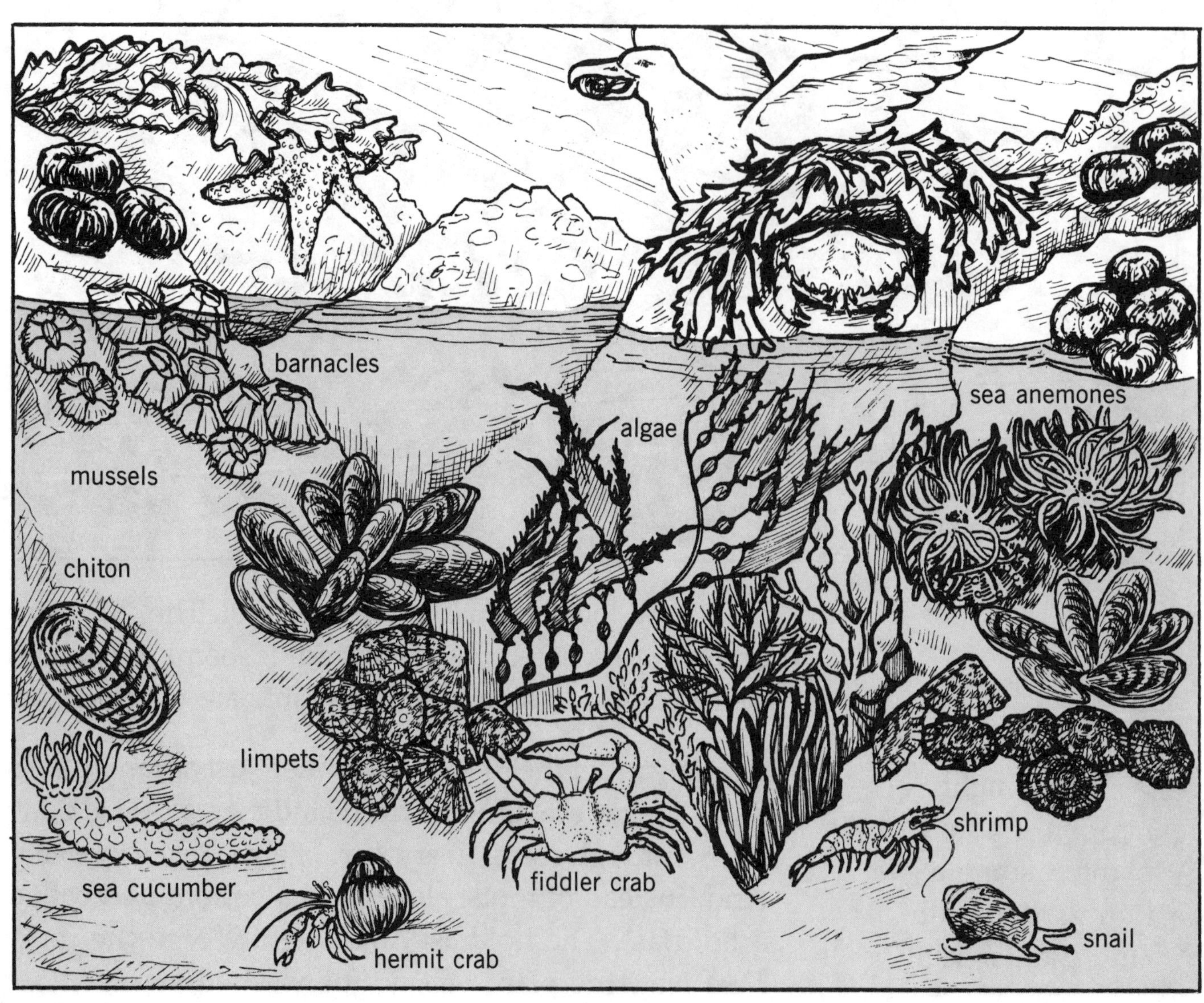

Think About It

▷ Why do the animals move to the bottom of the pool when the tide is low?

Students may note that mobile animals move to the wettest, coolest part of the pool for greater safety.

For the question below: Mussels are unable to escape predators because they are cemented to a rock. Explain that this is an example of cause and effect: Because the mussel is attached to the rock, it cannot escape predators.

Think About It

▷ Why can't a mussel get away from a sea star?

Soon the tide will come in and cover these rocks. Pretend that you are here then. You see waves pour in and water cover the pool. The waves carry **plankton,** a kind of "sea soup." Plankton is mostly made up of millions of tiny plants. The eggs of sea creatures and animals so small you can't see them are also in it.

Now the mussels open their shells. They suck in the sea soup and spit out the water. This is how mussels get the food they need. Barnacles get their food in a different way. The top of a barnacle opens. Arms like feathers come out. Its 12 arms pull plankton inside.

You watch as a sea star climbs over the mussel bed. It throws its strong arms around a mussel. Then it tries to pull apart the mussel's shell. The mussel tries to hold its shell closed. After a long fight, the sea star wins. The sea star sends its stomach out through its mouth and into the opened shell. Then the sea star sucks out the mussel's insides.

Think About It

▷ How are a mussel and a crab alike? How are they different?

A crab looks for food carried in on the tide. It will eat any animal—even other crabs. It grabs a big shrimp and begins to tear it. All kinds of worms swim in the water, too. They are looking for smaller animals to eat. They are also trying to keep from becoming another animal's dinner.

Answers to these questions will vary. Possible responses include: They are alike in that they both look for food carried in by the tide, they both have shells, they both live in or near tide pools. They are different because while the crab moves about to get its food, the mussel waits for food to pass by in the tide.

With a shrimp chasing it, a glass worm comes too close to a sea anemone. When the tide came in and the water rose, the anemone opened up. Now it looks like a beautiful flower with yellow petals. The "petals" catch the worm and sting it. Then the anemone pushes the worm into its mouth under the petals.

For the question below, help students articulate their answers by modeling a comparison: At high tide the beach is covered by water, but at low tide part of the beach is dry. Have students then make other comparisons about animal activity and so on.

Think About It

▷ How is the rocky beach at high tide different from the beach at low tide?

In the dark pool, every animal is busy getting food. By low tide, each will have eaten. Or it will have been eaten. Each living thing helps the rest go on living.

Take a last look for today at the tide pool. Much will happen here when night comes and the tide comes in. Yet tomorrow everything will look almost the same to you. That is because as some animals die, others take their place. In this way, this small world is like our own larger world. As long as we do not hurt it, this beautiful place will go on being home to many different animals for a long time to come.

2 After reading *"Land's End"*

Think about the story

1. Could you really stay and watch what happens in a tide pool after the tide comes in? Why or why not?

Students will probably recognize that the tide pool would be covered with water, making observation difficult without special equipment. Some students may conclude from the text that darkness would also present problems. Clarify that because tidal flows are a half hour later each day and there are two tides each day, at least one tide occurs during daylight hours almost every day. You may want to discuss the importance of staying off rocks where waves are breaking, particularly when the tide is rising.

2. In a tidepool, what eats what? Think about the creatures named below. Then write some sentences telling which eats what.

plankton **mussels** **sea star**

Students may note that plankton is eaten by mussels, and mussels may be eaten by sea stars. You might point out that the relationship among these three creatures represents part of a food chain.

3. Name one animal that moves around in a tidepool. How does it feed itself?

Answers will vary. You may want to assist students by asking them to recall which animals can and cannot move about. Then have students select one of each and describe how it feeds. Possible responses include: A starfish can move around. It feeds on mussels by squeezing the shells open.

Name one animal that stays in one place in a tidepool. How does it feed itself?

A barnacle can't move around. It feeds by opening its shell and sucking in plankton. Encourage students to look back at the selection to confirm their answers.

4. Finish this table. What does each animal do at low and high tide?

	HIGH TIDE	LOW TIDE
limpet	moves across rock to eat	closes up tight
barnacle	top opens; twelve arms come out and pull in plankton	sticks itself to rock in one place
sea anemone	opens up; stings animals with its "petals"	closes up into a bump

Check what you learned

Turn back to page 13. Read again what you wanted to learn from this story. Did you find out what you wanted to know? If so, tell what you learned.

Answers will vary depending on the goals students set for themselves.

Were all your questions answered? If not, tell how you could find the answers.

Students may mention going to the library as a way of finding answers to their questions. You might arrange or suggest a visit to an aquarium if there is one in your community. In addition, have students read the titles of the books listed at the bottom of this page.

Use your own words

Imagine that you are a tide pool animal. You can be any animal you want. Write a story about a few hours in your day. Tell what you see and do. Use a separate piece of paper to write about what you do during these times:

- When the tide comes in
- When you spot an enemy
- When the tide goes out again

You may want students to follow the steps of the writing process described on page T10 of this Annotated Teacher's Edition to complete this activity. Invite students to read aloud their finished work. Students might also enjoy miming the movements and activities of the tide pool animals they wrote about.

Find out more

Did you enjoy "Land's End"? If so, read more about tide pool animals. Look for these books in your library:

- Bendick, Jeanne. *Exploring an Ocean Tide Pool.* Garrard Publishing Company, 1976.
- Mainig, Anita. *Where the Waves Break: Life at the Edge of the Sea.* Carolrhoda Books, 1985.
- Podendorf, Illa. *Animals of the Sea and Shore.* Children's Press, 1982.

3 Before reading *"The Way It Used to Be"*

Think of what you know

You already know many things that help you when you read. What do you know about whales? How did people use whales long ago? Talk about your ideas. Then write what you think this story will be about.

This selection focuses on nineteenth-century whaling through a young sailor's experiences on his first whale hunt. It goes on to describe New Bedford, Massachusetts, the most important whaling port in the world in the mid-1800s, and the people who made their living from the whaling industry. The main product, whale oil, was used for candles, soap, and lantern oil, among other things. Finally, the decline of the whaling industry and the popular feeling that all remaining whales should be protected are summarized. Discuss sailing, sailing ships, and what experiences a person can expect when taking a long trip at sea. Students may predict the selection will be about hunting or watching whales.

Decide what you want to learn

Always read with questions in mind. Then you can look for answers to them. Look at the picture on page 22. How does it make you feel?

The picture shows nineteenth-century whalers attacking their prey on the high seas. Students may note the danger involved in whaling or express horror at the slaughter of whales.

Write one thing you hope to learn from this story.

Students may want to know why whales were (are) hunted and killed.

Get ready to use your reading skills

As you read, you need to put facts together. Sometimes a story does not tell you how all the facts fit. The questions in the green boxes will help you. They ask you to think about:

Why things happen. Can you figure out why something happens in the story? Can you see what happens because of it?

Your own thoughts. Can your own thoughts help you judge what the story says?

How things go together. Can you use facts and ideas you already know to help you understand new ideas?

Understand the words

Here are some words from "The Way It Used to Be." Use the story and pictures to help you understand them.

barrels	**harpoon**	**risk**
builders	**inns**	**spear**
coopers	**mast**	**whaleman**

To help students with new vocabulary, create a semantic map around the word *whaling*. You might begin by drawing the outline of a whale on the chalkboard and discussing the characteristics of whales. Then help students understand how each new word might be used in talking about whaling.

3 Reading

The Way It Used to Be

A young sailor stood high in a lookout's nest at the top of his ship's mast. He looked out across the water. Suddenly, he saw a tall fountain of spray. A whale was blowing water into the air. "Thar she blows!" he cried. Men began to run across the deck below him. They jumped into small boats that were being dropped over the side of the ship. The sailor climbed down the mast and joined them.

Think About It

▷ What do you think the sailors are going to do?

Answers will vary. Students will probably predict that the sailors are going to go after the whale to try to kill it.

The boats hit the water. The sailors began to row toward a large gray shape. It was the whale. The men in the boats were setting off to kill it.

THE SPERM WHALE IN A FLURRY.

One man stood in the front of each boat. He held a sharp, heavy spear called a **harpoon.** The boats neared the whale. The young sailor could hear the soft sound of the giant animal's breath. Through the sea spray just ahead, he could see the whale. He had never seen anything so big. He had never been so scared, either.

Then the harpooners threw with all their might. The harpoons stuck deep in the whale's head. Badly hurt, the animal dived, trying to get away. Its tail pounded the water and almost hit the young sailor's boat. The whale dived again. But the harpoons were tied to ropes curled in the bottom of the boats. The whale could not get away. The sea ran red with its blood.

Think About It

▷ Think about a whaleman's job. What do you think the job was like?

The young whaleman knew he had to help kill many more whales. The ship had to be filled with barrels of whale oil before it could sail for home. Some ships were at sea for five years. So there were many long days with nothing to do. The young sailor often sat with the other men. They would carve pictures on the bones of the whales they had killed. He carved things for his mother's kitchen and dreamed of being back home again.

Answers will vary. Possible responses include: dangerous, boring, exciting. You may want to model for students how they can use information from the selection along with what they know to make judgments about what they read.

Home was New Bedford, a town on the rocky edge of Buzzard's Bay in Massachusetts. The young man dreamed of his family's little gray house. He could almost smell the wild roses. He dreamed of apple trees heavy with fruit. But when he was a boy, he had dreamed of going to sea.

The young man went off whaling in 1850. At that time New Bedford was the most important whaling city in the world. The harbor was deep enough for the sailing ships. Hundreds of New Bedford men were whalemen.

Think About It

▷ Do you think New Bedford was an interesting place to live in 1850? Why or why not?

Answers will vary. Encourage students to use details from the selection, as well as what they already know, to justify their opinions. Help students to conclude that New Bedford was an interesting place because of the variety of people from different cultures gathered there.

For the question below: Yes, because the whaling industry created many jobs for people from boat builders to sail makers to coopers to innkeepers. You may want to call students' attention to the cause/effect relationship here.

Think About It

▷ Would New Bedford have been a good place to go to find work? Why or why not?

Whalemen from all over the world came to New Bedford. They came from Africa, India, Portugal, and South Sea Islands. Some had brightly colored birds sitting on their shoulders. Others carried walking sticks made of a whale's bone. They dressed in clothes of many colors. They were nothing like the New Bedford men, who dressed in brown and black.

Why would men go so far from home and risk their lives to kill whales? The answer was on the docks and in the streets of New Bedford. Barrels of whale oil lined the docks. Some of these were rolled into a "candle works" to be made into candles. Other barrels of oil were made into soap. Still others were used to heat stoves and light lamps. Whale oil gave the brightest, cleanest light in the world. Most people used to read by the light of whale oil lamps.

Many people in New Bedford worked on the whaling ships. Boat builders cut and sawed wood into boards. Then they hammered and fit the wooden boards to shape the beautiful ships. In big rooms, men made yards and yards of heavy cloth into sails. Other men fixed the sails onto the ships. Coopers made the barrels that held the oil. Inns sold food and drink and a place to sleep to the whalemen. The whole town made money from the killing of whales.

Think About It

▷ Why is whaling no longer important to the people of New Bedford?

Students may note that whale oil is no longer used to heat and light homes. Things that came from whales can now be made from other materials. Disapproval of whaling may also have helped cause its decline.

Think About It

▷ Do you think it is important for people to protect whales? Why or why not?

No one in New Bedford makes a living from killing whales anymore. We no longer need whale oil to make our homes warm or give us light. And all the other things that once came from whales can now be made from other things. But the town has not forgotten the brave young whaleman. Today a museum stands on Johnny Cake Hill. There people can see the things the young man carved for his mother's kitchen.

Many people now think whales should not be killed at all. But a few countries still send their ships to kill them. In fact, more whales have been killed in the last 50 years than in the 400 years before. Because the killing still goes on, some kinds of whales may soon be gone forever. Most people want to keep this from happening. They know the world would lose something wonderful if these beautiful giants no longer swam the seas.

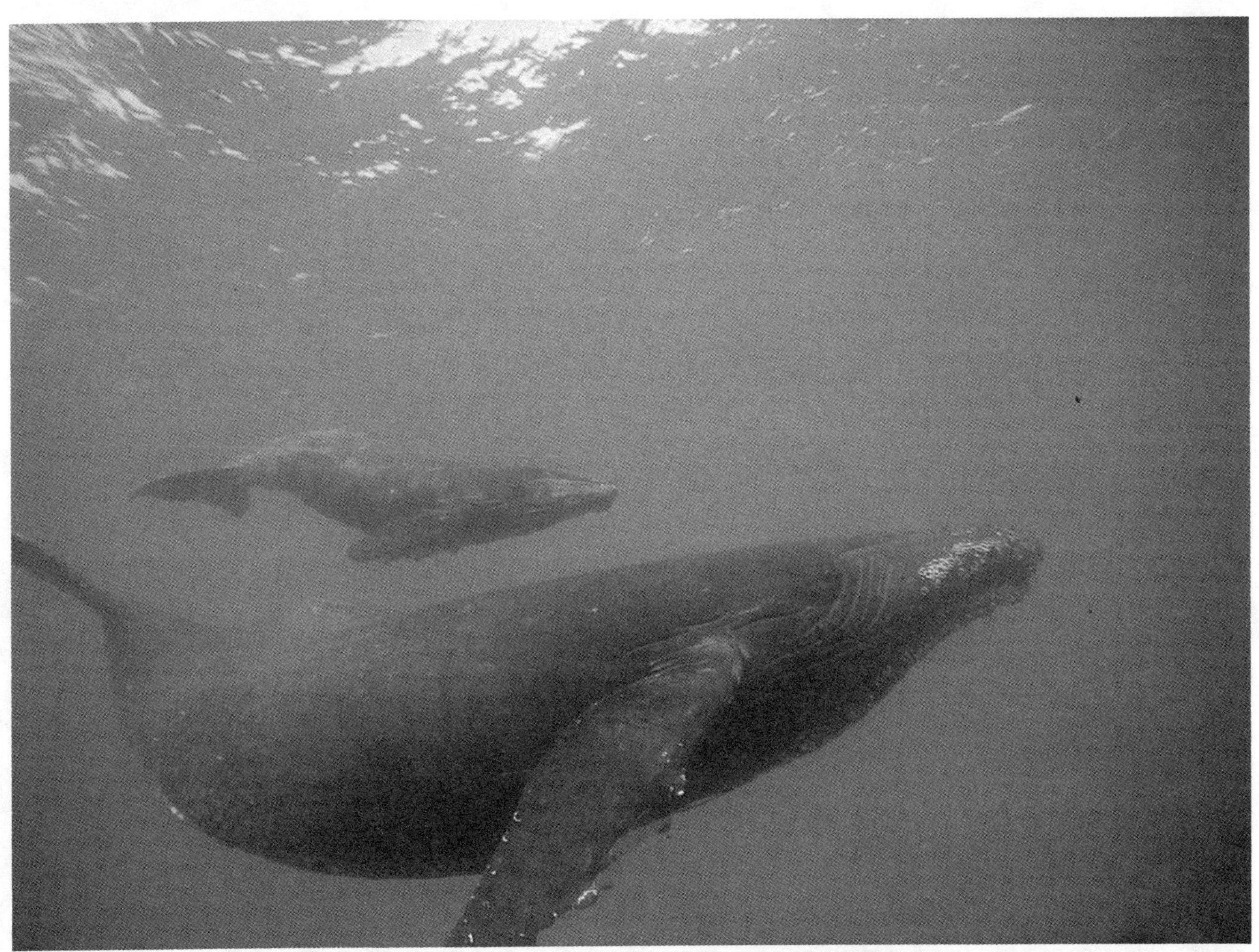

Answers will vary. You may want to model using details from the selection (*more whales have been killed in the last 50 years than in the 400 years before*) to help students make an informed judgment about whether the world's whale population needs protection.

3 After reading *"The Way It Used to Be"*

Think about the story

1. Pretend that you could walk down the streets of New Bedford in 1850. What are some of the things you might see?

Answers will vary. Students are likely to mention things shown in the pictures on pages 23 and 24. They may also mention sail makers' workshops, inns, shops, homes, etc. Help students compare and contrast the look of a port city in the 1850s with one today.

2. Tell why whaling was so important for the people of New Bedford.

Answers will vary. Encourage students to demonstrate an understanding that many people in New Bedford depended on whaling and the industries associated with it for their livelihoods. Help students recognize that New Bedford's development as a whaling port was caused by its good harbor and hardworking whalemen.

3. Why do you think the people of New Bedford want to remember the whalemen of long ago?

Answers will vary. You might want to lead a discussion of local history and why people preserve items from the past both in their homes and in museums. Invite students to tell why it is important to remember their own local heroes.

4. Think about the people below. Then fill in the chart. Show who did what in New Bedford.

cooper **boat builder** **soap maker** **sailor**
whaleman **candle maker** **sail maker** **mast builder**

Built ships	Hunted whales	Made barrels to store whale oil	Made things from whale oil
boat builder mast builder sail maker	whalemen sailor	cooper	soap maker candle maker

Check what you learned

Turn back to page 21. Read again what you wanted to learn from this story. Did you find out what you wanted to know? If so, tell what you learned.

Answers will vary depending on the goals students set for themselves.

Were all your questions answered? If not, tell how you could find the answers.

Students may mention going to the library as a way to find answers to their questions. In addition, have students read the titles of the books suggested at the bottom of this page.

Use your own words

Pretend you are a whaleman in New Bedford. Write about a whaling trip. Use a separate piece of paper and try to answer these questions:

- How long have you been gone?
- How many whales have you seen?
- What is it like to hunt a whale?
- What do you like and not like about living on a ship?

Find out more

Did you enjoy "The Way It Used to Be"? If so, read more about life long ago and about whales. Look for these books in your library:

- Hall, Donald. *Ox-cart Man.* Viking Press, 1979.
- Knight, James E. *Salem Days: Life in a Colonial Seaport.* Troll Associates, 1982.
- Patent, Dorthy Hinshaw. *All About Whales.* Holiday House, 1987.

When students have finished their accounts of a whaling trip, suggest that they illustrate their writing. Then arrange a display of students' work in the classroom.

4 Before reading *"Hurricane!"*

Think of what you know

You already know many things that help you when you read. What do you know about hurricanes? Have you ever been near one or seen pictures of one on TV? Talk about your ideas. Then write what you think this story will be about.

This selection describes the devastation created in New England by the great hurricane of 1938. Then the formation and growth of hurricanes are explained. Finally, the techniques of meteorologists in predicting and tracking hurricanes are summarized. Lead the students in a discussion of storms or natural disasters that occur in your region. Students may predict that the selection will tell about the damage caused by hurricanes.

Decide what you want to learn

Always read with questions in mind. Then you can look for answers to them. Look at the picture on page 29. What do you see?

The photograph shows the effects of Hurricane Hugo on a coastal community.

Write one thing you hope to learn from this story.

Students may want to know what causes hurricanes.

Get ready to use your reading skills

As you read, you need to put facts together. Sometimes a story does not tell you how all the facts fit. The questions in the green boxes will help you. They ask you to think about:

What people are feeling. Can you put yourself in another person's place? Can you imagine what that person feels or thinks?

Where the facts lead. You already know some facts. Others are given in the story. Can you put them together to figure out new ideas?

What the most important idea is. Can you find a sentence that tells the most important idea of the story?

Understand the words

Here are some words from "Hurricane!" Use the story and pictures to help you understand them.

dangerous	**nature**	**shelter**
donut	**pilot**	**spiral**
hurricane	**satellites**	**watchers**

To help students with the new vocabulary, divide them into small groups. Give each group one of the words to define and illustrate. When the students have finished, invite a volunteer from each group to present that group's work to the class.

4 Reading

Hurricane!

Answers for the question below will vary. Most students are likely to predict that the selection will be about the deaths and destruction caused by hurricanes.

Think About It

▷ What do you think this story will be about?

It was the third week of September, 1938. Along the Atlantic coast of the United States, people were enjoying the last warm days of summer. The radio said to get ready for rain. But people did not really listen. Some kept swimming or stayed on the beaches.

A huge storm had formed at sea. At first it seemed to be headed for land. But it had missed Florida and then the Carolinas. Maybe it had gone back out to sea.

Finally, on September 21 the storm hit. A wave 18 feet high struck Long Island in New York. It washed away the beaches there. People in the water were carried out to sea. Old trees were cut in half. Younger ones were pulled up by the roots. The storm hit town after town. One town had 179 houses before the storm. Only 12 were left standing. In Sag Harbor, a tall church tower was snapped off like a twig.

After Long Island, the storm struck the coast of Connecticut. Boats were tossed along streets. Some crashed into houses. Train tracks were twisted like string. Huge waves flooded whole towns. On Block Island, the storm ruined all the fishing boats.

Think About It

▷ Why did the 1938 storm hurt so many people?

▷ What do you think might have helped?

Answers for the first two questions above will vary. Possible responses include: The 1938 storm hurt so many people because

Think About It

▷ What makes hurricanes so harmful?

it moved very fast across a large area; people could have prepared for it more effectively if they had known beforehand how serious the storm was going to be.

For the question in the second box: Hurricanes are very large and can destroy almost everything in their path.

The storm then raced through Massachusetts, New Hampshire, and Maine. Telephone poles and power lines blew down. The high winds knocked down hundreds of fruit trees, too. Many people died. On Mount Washington, in New Hampshire, the wind blew 190 miles an hour. It was the strongest wind ever measured there.

This terrible storm was a hurricane.

Hurricanes can do more harm than anything in nature. This is because hurricanes are so large. The donut shape of a hurricane may be as much as 500 miles wide. Its rain clouds may climb 5 to 10 miles into the air. The storm travels over sea and sometimes across land as well. A hurricane may travel 2,000 miles. Along the way, it hurts everything in its path.

Hurricanes need warm water to get started. Most begin out in the warm Atlantic Ocean. There, steady winds called **trade winds** blow west. Warmed by the ocean, the winds pick up water. The warm, wet wind starts to move up and make clouds. Cooler air rushes into its place. This cool air warms, picks up water, and rises, too. A great spiral of wind and clouds begins.

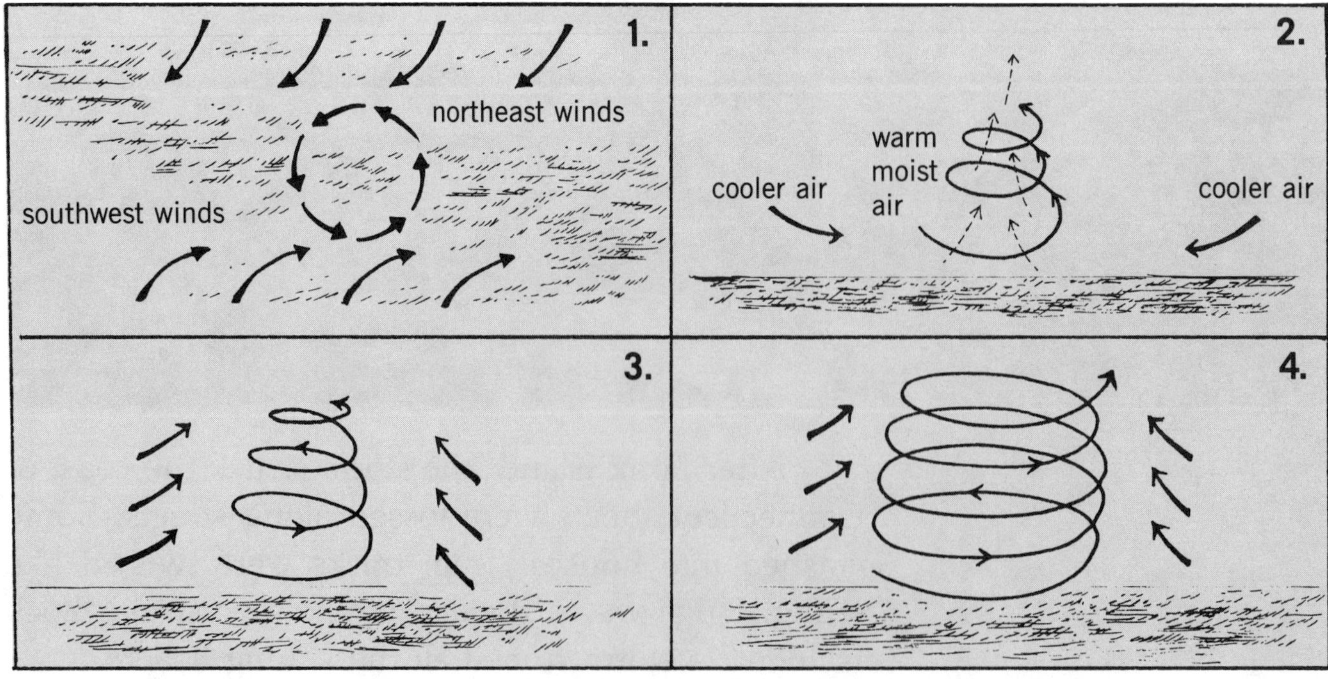

Think About It

▷ Why do you think hurricanes happen mostly in summer?

Hurricanes need warm water to form, so they are more likely to occur in the warm summer season. You may want to model how students can use facts from the story along with what they already know to arrive at the answer to this question.

The clouds grow bigger and wetter. Huge walls of rain form. The wind blows faster and faster. When the winds reach 74 miles an hour, the storm becomes a hurricane. Some grow so large that their winds roar at 200 miles an hour.

Many hurricanes stay out at sea. They hurt only ships. But some hurricanes move toward the land. Their winds push sea water toward shore. Waves as high as 50 feet can wash whole beaches away. They may slam into Gulf states such as Texas, Louisiana, and Florida. They can flood cities along the Atlantic coast from Florida to Maine.

Hurricanes happen every year. About ten of them form over the Atlantic Ocean each summer. Some move west and hit land. There is no way to stop them. What can people do? The best way to keep safe from a hurricane is to know about it early. Know when it's coming and how strong it is. Then take shelter.

Think About It

▷ How do you think people feel when they hear that a hurricane is coming?

After the terrible hurricane of 1938, weather watchers worked hard to learn about new hurricanes early. Ships at sea sent them news by radio. People on islands sent word of new storms. In 1943, a pilot flew a plane into the middle of a hurricane for the first time. This was very dangerous. But it was the only way to measure the winds and the rain. Weather watchers learned more with each storm.

Answers will vary. Some students may think that having a hurricane approach would be exciting, while others may think it would be terrifying. You may want to model putting yourself in another person's place to help students imagine how someone else might feel.

In 1955, a National Hurricane Center opened. It gathered reports about hurricanes. Then it told all the towns and cities in the path of each storm what could happen.

Today, hurricanes are not surprises. Satellites high above the earth take pictures of the oceans. They spot any large clouds that take the shape of a ring. Hour by hour, weather watchers keep track of the clouds. They watch to see if the clouds are growing. They see which way the storm moves. Sometimes they send a weather plane into its "eye." This is the calm place at the center of the storm. The plane picks up signals of how bad the storm may be.

Think About It

▷ The National Hurricane Center began its work in 1955. How do you think it has helped people since then?

Knowing beforehand about a hurricane allows people to better protect themselves and their belongings from the storm's destructive forces. You may want to model using story facts along with prior knowledge to draw conclusions that help students answer this question.

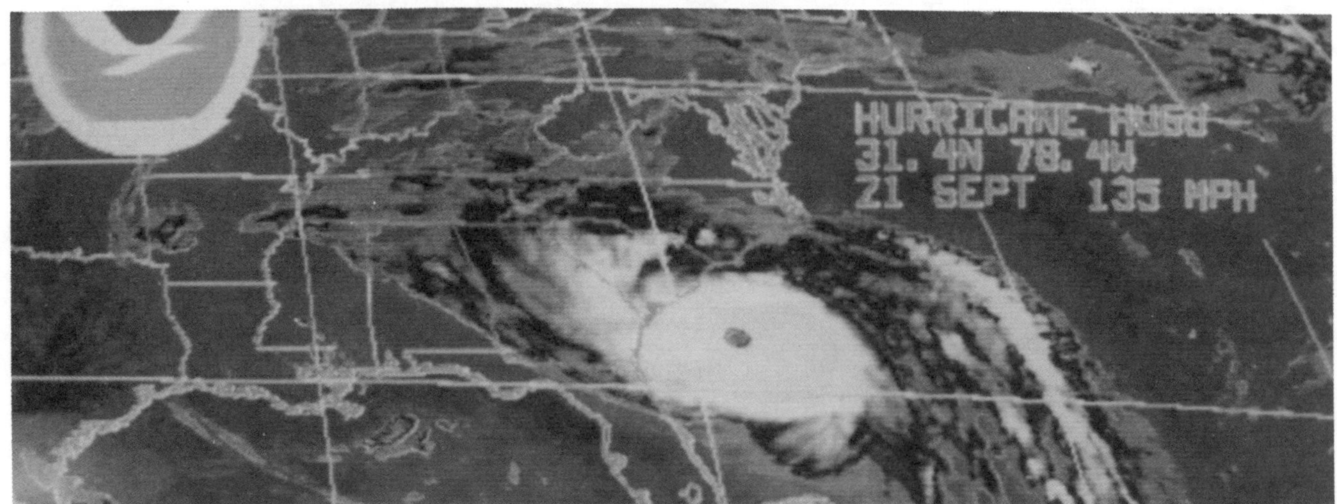

Weather watchers speak on radio and TV. They tell people in towns and cities to get ready for the storm. People cover windows with boards and tie things down. They sail their boats back to shore. Most important, people move far from the beaches. They stay away until the storm passes.

Hurricanes still do terrible harm. But weather watchers have been a big help. In 1961, they told people in the Gulf states about Hurricane Carla. More than 350,000 people moved away from the coast. When Carla blew into Texas with winds up to 180 miles an hour, it knocked down everything in its path. Yet few people were killed. The weather watchers had done their job.

Think About It

▷ Why do you think people tie things down in a hurricane? Why do they move away from shore?

Answers to these questions may vary. Possible responses include: People tie things down to keep them from being picked up and blown away or destroyed by the strong winds; people move away from the shore because the waves created by the storm crash into the shore, so they move inland to protect themselves.

4 After reading *"Hurricane!"*

Think about the story

1. The picture on page 30 shows how a hurricane begins. Use it to help you put the steps below in order. Write the numbers *1* to *4* on the lines to show the order.

   __4__ The hurricane moves west toward land.

   __1__ Trade winds blow from east to west.

   __3__ The whirling wind grows to 500 miles wide.

   __2__ Cooler air blows in, warms, and spins upward.

After students complete the activity, have them confirm or correct their responses by discussing them with classmates.

2. Suppose you want to tell someone else about hurricanes. What are the most important ideas you should explain?

Answers will vary. Some students will focus on hurricane danger. Some will focus on the size and strength of the hurricane, or the precautions people take before a hurricane. Guide students to differentiate between these main ideas and their supporting details.

3. Hurricanes strike beaches and towns in Florida or the Gulf states every few years. Why do you think people live in places that can be dangerous?

Answers will vary. You might organize a debate about whether or not it is sensible to live in a hurricane region. To help students see both sides, have them try to take the position of the side opposite their own.

4. Suppose you had the chance to fly in a plane into a hurricane. Would you do it? Explain why or why not.

Answers will vary. Some students are likely to say such a flight sounds thrilling, while others will say it sounds horrifying. Invite students to explain their reactions. Then discuss the goal of such flights—to gather information.

Check what you learned

Turn back to page 28. Read again what you wanted to learn from this story. Did you find out what you wanted to know? If so, tell what you learned.

Answers will vary depending on the goals students set for themselves.

Were all your questions answered? If not, tell how you could find the answers.

Have students complete this activity independently and share their answers. Then have students work in groups to pose additional questions they would like to answer and conduct the research to do so. Some students might enjoy researching a related topic such as tornadoes, earthquakes, or droughts.

Use your own words

Imagine you are in a beach house on the Atlantic coast. Your radio has not been working for a week. Finally your family gets it fixed. The first thing you hear is a hurricane warning. It is too late to drive away safely. You have to sit out the storm in your house. Write about your adventure. Use a separate piece of paper and try to answer these questions:

- What did you do to get ready for the storm?
- What did it feel like when the storm struck?
- What did you do during the storm?
- When the storm was over, what did you do?
- What did you see when you looked outside?

Invite students to share their adventures with the class.

Find out more

Did you enjoy "Hurricane"? If so, read more about these storms. Look for these books in your library:

- Branley, Franklyn M. *Hurricane Watch.* Crowell, 1985.
- Fradin, Dennis B. *Disaster! Hurricanes.* Children's Press, 1982.

After reading *COMMUNITIES BY THE SEA*

Think about what you've learned

Read each question. Fill in the circle next to the best answer.

1. People on both land and sea fear these.
   - (A) trawlers
   - (B) barnacles
   - (C) hurricanes
   - (D) harpoons

2. What makes barnacles open and close?
   - (A) day and night
   - (B) spring and fall
   - (C) warm and cold air
   - (D) high and low tide

3. Every city by the sea where boats go in and out has one of these.
   - (A) harpoon
   - (B) satellite
   - (C) harbor
   - (D) trawler

4. A *trawler* is
   - (A) a fishing boat with a net.
   - (B) a fishing boat with harpoons.
   - (C) a person who makes barrels.
   - (D) a whaleman.

Read each question. Write your answer on the lines.

5. What are some "gifts" the sea has given to the people who live near it?

Answers will vary. Possible responses include: food; jobs, including fishing, processing fish, selling fish, cooking fish, building boats, repairing boats; entertainment, including playing and swimming at the beach, going for long walks along the shore; awareness of nature, including studying creatures in a tide pool, watching whales or sea lions swimming, digging for clams; etc. Encourage students to explain their choice of gifts.

6. You read about Gloucester today and New Bedford 200 years ago. Which city would you rather live in? Why?

Answers will vary greatly. Make sure students' explanations are plausible and justify their choice.

Write about what you've learned

People who live near the sea must be careful for their own safety. They also must take care of the sea and its creatures. How can they do these things? Use a separate piece of paper to write your ideas.

You might want to have students follow the steps of the writing process described on page T10 of this Annotated Teacher's Edition to complete this activity. First, have students brainstorm lists of safety rules for people and ways to maintain sea life. Write the suggestions on the chalkboard and urge students to consult them as they write. When they have finished, invite students to illustrate their ideas. Then make a book of the students' essays and pictures. Have the class vote on a title for their book.

UNIT **Two**

LIVING IN CITIES

To start:
When Henry Hudson first reached the island of Manhattan in 1609, Algonquin Indians were living along the banks of the Hudson and East rivers. The Netherlands claimed the island, and Dutch colonists arrived there in 1624, laying out a town and fort at the southern tip. In 1626, the governor, Peter Minuit, gave the Algonquins about $24 worth of goods to buy the whole island.

Today New York City comprises five boroughs: the Bronx, Brooklyn, Staten Island, Queens, and Manhattan. With over 7 million people, it is the largest city in the U.S. and a vital world center of business, trade, culture, and diplomacy. Ask students *You already know something about living in cities* to tell what they know about New York City.

It is a hot summer day in 1626. The young Native American woman stands with her friends in the grassy clearing. They have come to talk to the pale strangers from across the sea. The strangers want to buy this island of Manhates.

On this island are forests full of animals. Wild fruits grow in the meadows. The rivers and ponds are full of fish. So why not sell this land to the strangers? There is enough land for all. Besides, the cloth the strangers offer is soft. And the beads are beautiful. The sun shines right through them.

Now, it is a hot summer day in the 1990s. A young woman stands on the same spot. But she stands on a sidewalk, not grass. People rush past. Horns honk, people shout, and trucks roar by. All around the woman are huge buildings that seem to touch the sky. Ships sail in and out of the harbor. This island is now one of the world's great cities. It is New York City, on the island of Manhattan.

Think. Write some words that tell about living in cities.

Answers will vary. Possibilities include: skyscrapers, apartment houses, buses, crowds, stores and shops, noise, movies and theater, zoo, etc.

Talk. Share your ideas. Talk with a few classmates. See who can answer these questions:

- How many big cities can you name?
- How is living in a city different from living in the country?
- What makes cities grow and change?

Students may name New York, Chicago, Los Angeles, Houston, Miami, etc.; note that life in a city is faster, more crowded, noisier, and more exciting; and say that cities grow and change as people come and go.

Write. What are some good things and some bad things about living in cities? Write your ideas on another piece of paper.

Encourage students to share their writing with the class. List their ideas on the chalkboard in two columns labeled **Good Things in Cities** and **Bad Things in Cities.** After students have completed the unit, you may want them to see if they have changed their minds about the lists—or the headings—as a result of their reading.

New words, new uses

Some of the words in this unit may be new to you. Keep them in mind as you read the stories to come.

energy: the power used by people
fossil: remains of a plant or animal from an earlier time
harbor: a safe place where ships can stop
settle: to move in and then stay in a place
survive: to stay alive

Predicting

Here are the names of the stories in Unit Two. Read them and look at the picture below. Then write three things you think you might learn from the stories.

How Does a City Grow? *A City's Bones*
Wildlife in the City *Plugging into Power*

Students will learn about: (1) the founding and growth of St. Augustine, Florida, and Chicago, Illinois; (2) the adaptation of wild animals to an urban environment; (3) the fossils found in the La Brea Tar Pits; and (4) the sources and production of the electricity cities need in order to function.

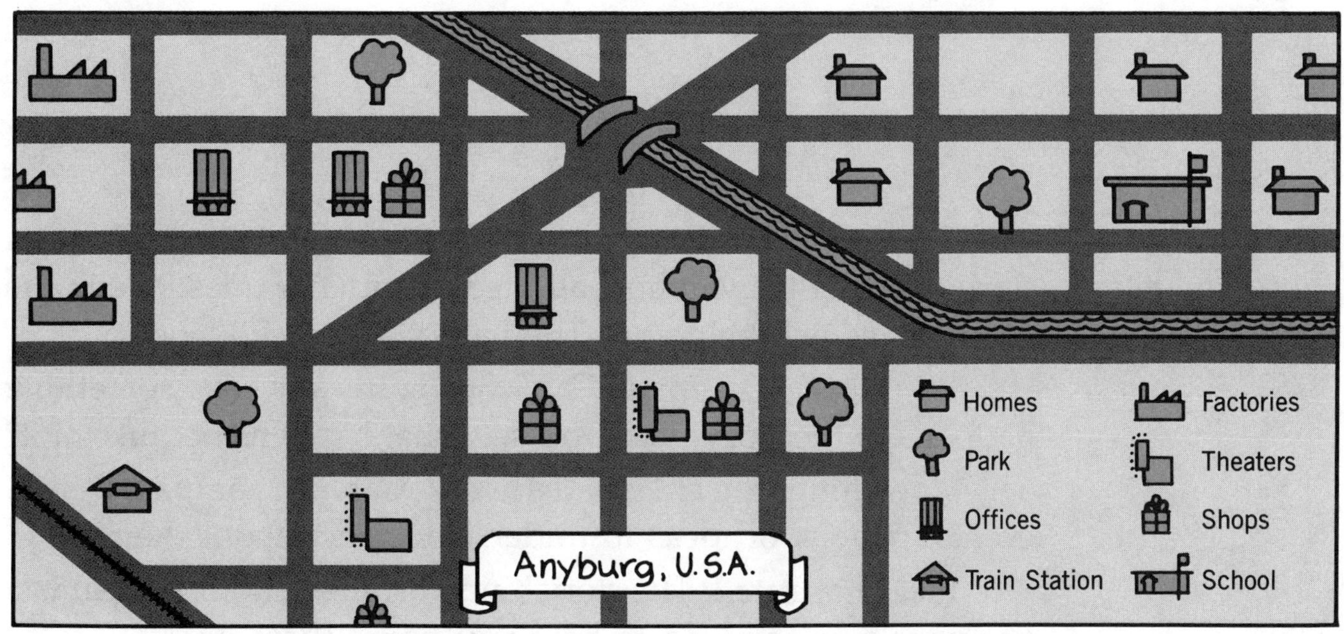

New information

After you have finished this unit, you will know the answers to these questions and more:

- What makes a city grow and change?
- How can wild animals live in big cities?
- What creatures lived long ago where cities stand today?
- What makes the lights go on in a city?

Have students examine and comment on the map on this page. You might help them to compare the layout of "Anyburg" with that of your own community. Explain that the map is not of a real city and therefore doesn't show all the features of a real city. Give students an opportunity to add more symbols to the map key and map (for example, municipal buildings, police and fire stations, hospital, etc.).

1 Before reading *"How Does a City Grow?"*

Think of what you know

You already know many things that help you when you read. Why do people settle in one place and not another? Why do they stay? How did your own town or city begin? Talk about your ideas. Then write what you think this story will be about.

This selection begins with the founding by Spaniards of St. Augustine, Florida, in 1565 and goes on to explain the city's relatively small size despite its age. The selection then moves on to cite factors, such as natural resources and location, that help cities grow. It examines the founding and growth of Chicago and finally notes that all cities are alike in providing homes to people. Discuss with students why some spots are better for cities than others. Share with them what you know about the origin of your own community.

Decide what you want to learn

Always read with questions in mind. Then you can look for answers to them. Look at the picture on page 39. What do you think it shows?

The Spanish admiral, Pedro Menendez de Aviles, peers through his telescope at the land that would become St. Augustine, Florida.

Write one thing you hope to learn from this story.

Students may want to know why some cities grow and others do not.

Get ready to use your reading skills

As you read, you need to put facts together. Sometimes a story does not tell you how all the facts fit. The questions in the green boxes will help you. They ask you to think about:

Why things happen. Can you figure out why something happens in the story? Can you see what happens because of it?

How things are alike or different. Can you compare things, events, people, or ideas to understand more about them?

Ideas not stated. The story hints at some new ideas. Can you use your own thinking to help you figure them out?

Understand the words

Here are some words from "How Does a City Grow?" Use the story and pictures to help you understand them.

admiral	**location**	**settle**
canal	**mill**	**telescope**
future	**natural resources**	**trading post**

To help students with new vocabulary, have them work with a partner to define one of the new terms and then illustrate it in a context that relates to human settlement. When students have finished, call on volunteer partners to present their work to the class until all the words have been discussed.

1 Reading

How Does a City Grow?

It was August of 1565. Some wooden ships bobbed up and down in the Atlantic Ocean near Florida. Sailors from three of the ships had already landed. They found trees on shore, and fresh water. The sailors still on the ships longed to join their friends. The heat was terrible. When would the captain give the word for the rest of them to land?

Possible response to the question below: He probably felt good about it because he could see it had all the features needed to start a settlement: deep water for ships, wood, water, level land with good soil, etc.

On the bridge of the biggest ship, Admiral Pedro Menendez de Aviles was not thinking of today's heat. He was thinking of tomorrow, and the years to come. He was trying to see into the future.

The admiral stared through his telescope. His ships were just outside Matanzas Bay. He saw a fine harbor there. He saw streams and trees with good wood. Here and there the forest gave way to open, flat land with rich, green grass.

Think About It

▷ How do you think Admiral Menendez de Aviles felt about the land he saw through his telescope?

In his mind the admiral could see Spaniards planting seeds on the open land and caring for cattle. He saw them cutting down trees and building homes. He saw ships in the harbor proudly flying the flag of Spain.

Admiral Menendez made up his mind. He gave the order to land. This would be a good place for people to live.

Can people really see into the future? Maybe Pedro Menendez de Aviles was one person who could. The town he and his sailors founded, St. Augustine, Florida, is now 425 years old. It was the first town built by Europeans in America.

Think About It

▷ Did the admiral choose a good place to land? How can you tell?

Answers will vary. Most students will probably say yes, because the town he founded has lasted 425 years.

Today many people visit this pretty place to look at the Spanish homes and other buildings built so long ago. St. Augustine is not a big city. Its people would agree with the admiral, though, that it is a good place to live.

Why aren't the oldest cities in America also the biggest? Why do some cities grow large and other cities stay small?

Cities grow where people want to live. And people have many different reasons for wanting to live in a place. People want to live where they can find work. **Natural resources,** such as water or trees or oil, are good reasons for choosing a place. Weather also helps people decide on a place to live. Where a city is, and what is around it, are also important. This is called **location.**

For the question below, encourage students to first think about how explorers traveled long ago. Have them consider why river travel might be better than land travel. (River travel was easier and faster than land travel.) Help students to understand that by crossing this narrow piece of land, explorers could continue to travel a long way by river.

Think About It

▷ Why was this portage so important for explorers?

One of the world's great cities grew near the southern end of Lake Michigan. Here, there is a low piece of land a few miles wide. It is called a **portage.** The portage lies between Lake Michigan and the Des Plaines River, which leads to the great Mississippi River.

Hundreds of years ago, French explorers came down into Lake Michigan from Canada in small boats. They carried the boats over this portage to get to the Des Plaines River. Once they reached the river, they could go all the way to the Mississippi. The explorers called this place "che-cau-gou." This was a Native American word for a wild plant that grew there. The modern city that now stands there is still called Chicago.

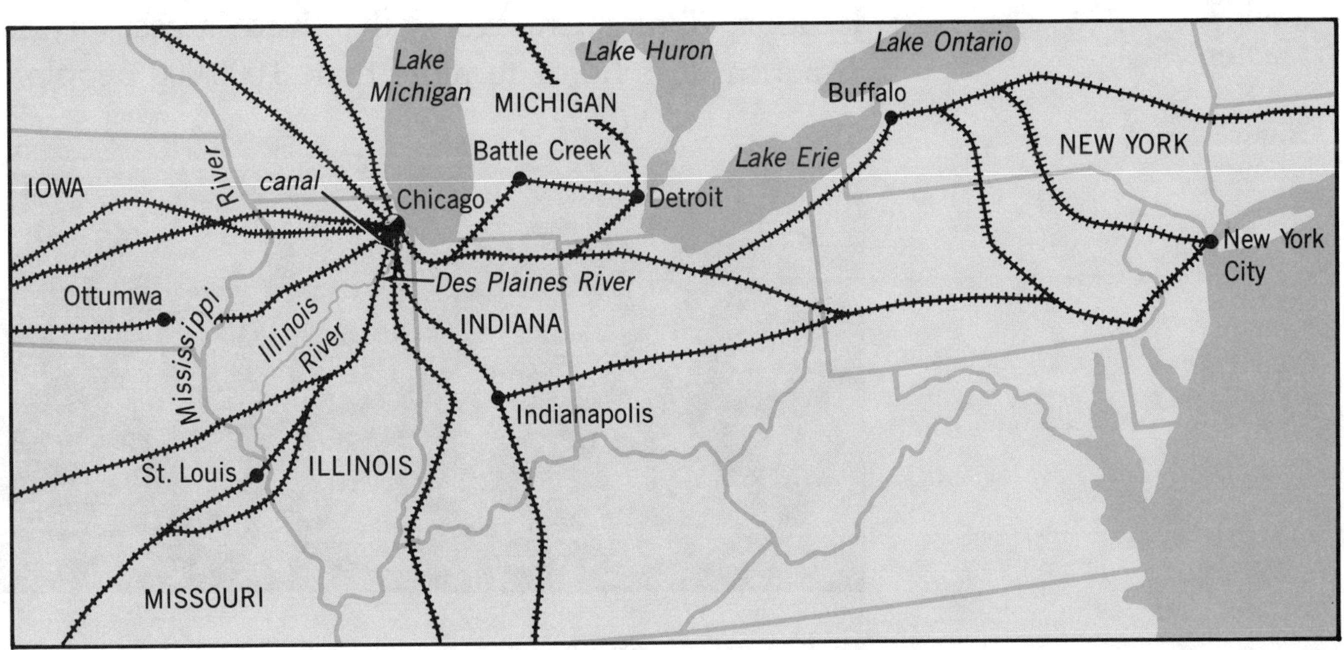

The first person to settle in Chicago was Jean Baptiste Point du Sable. No one knows just where he came from. People think his family came from France and Africa. In any case, he opened a trading post where the Chicago River meets Lake Michigan in 1779. He also married a Native American woman. Together they built a house and a mill where they made flour. He built a bakery, a barn, and shops to work in. Du Sable traded with the Native Americans and with other settlers. The city of Chicago was on its way.

Think About It

▷ Why do you think du Sable chose this spot for his trading post? What do you think he traded?

Answers will vary. Students will probably recall that the spot lay on an important route between Lake Michigan and the Mississippi River, so Du Sable's trading post would be in a good place to trade with people coming through. Based on what he had at his trading post, he most probably traded grain, bread, and livestock. He also certainly traded furs.

Possible response to the question below: The canal made it possible to move goods by water to the Mississippi River, which made Chicago accessible for even more of the country's commerce. This meant that more and more people would be needed to ensure the smooth flow of goods through Chicago to most parts of the U.S.

Think About It

▷ Look at the map on page 41. How did the canal help Chicago grow faster?

At first Chicago grew slowly. Between 1779 and 1829, few new settlers arrived. Then more settlers began to come. In 1835, there were about 3,000 people in the busy young city.

Soon, people decided to build a canal. It would join the Great Lakes and the Mississippi River. When the canal was finished in 1848, Chicago began to grow faster and faster.

Just 20 years later, Chicago was one of America's most important cities. Mills and factories gave jobs to people. Newly built railroads carried goods from Chicago to all parts of the country. The canal and railroads helped Chicago make the most of its great location. Today, Chicago is the third largest city in America. It is home to more than 3,000,000 people.

As you can see, cities grow and change for many reasons. Some, like St. Augustine, stay small. Others, like Chicago, grow to become big, important centers for trade and travel. But all cities are alike in one way. Cities are home to people.

Possible response to the question below: People still move to Chicago because there are jobs and opportunities there.

Think About It

▷ People still move to Chicago to settle. Why do you think this is so?

In 1565, Admiral Menendez dreamed of people planting seeds and building homes. Today, people still must plan how they want their city to grow. They decide where to build new factories, houses, shops, roads, and schools. People still need to work together to help make cities good places to live.

1 After reading *"How Does a City Grow?"*

Think about the story

1. Use the map on page 41 to answer the questions below. You will need different colored pencils for these questions. (HINT: Remember, everything needs to go through Chicago.)

   A. How could corn grown near Ottumwa, Iowa, get to New York City? Use a blue pencil to show the best route, or path, the corn could take.
   Students will probably draw a blue line along the railroad track from Ottumwa through Chicago to New York City.

   B. What are two ways cereal from Battle Creek, Michigan, could get to St. Louis, Missouri? Use a purple pencil to show one way and a red one to show the other. Possible answers: rail from Battle Creek to Chicago, rivers (Des Plaines, Illinois, Mississippi) to St. Louis; rail from Battle Creek through Chicago to St. Louis; rail from Battle Creek through Chicago to the Mississippi, then down to St. Louis.

   C. What is the best way to get cars from Detroit, Michigan, to Indianapolis, Indiana, for a race? Use an orange pencil to mark the route.
   Students will probably choose either the northern or southern rail route from Detroit to Chicago and then the most direct rail route to Indianapolis.

2. What are some reasons why people settle in a place?

Answers will vary. Possible reasons include: jobs, natural resources, location, weather, transportation, food sources, etc. Ask students to explain their responses.

3. Most cities, like Chicago, keep growing. But some big cities get smaller over time. Why might people move away from a city?

Answers will vary. Possibilities include: bad weather; change of job, or loss of job in a city; change in trade routes or transportation; desire for more peace and quiet, and less crime. Encourage students to relate their answers to their own personal experiences.

4. How are Chicago and St. Augustine alike? How are they different?

Answers will vary. Possible similarities: Both cities have useful natural resources, such as wood and water; both have good locations on the water. Possible differences: St. Augustine is much older, it hasn't grown as much, it is mainly a tourist town; Chicago is much bigger, it is a busy trade and manufacturing center, it is on a lake and several rivers, not the ocean.

Check what you learned

Turn back to page 38. Read again what you wanted to learn from this story. Did you find out what you wanted to know? If so, tell what you learned.

Answers will vary depending on the goals students set for themselves.

Were all your questions answered? If not, tell how you could find the answers.

Students may mention going to the library as a way to find answers to their questions. If possible, arrange or suggest a visit to a local museum or planning office. In addition, suggest that students read one or more of the books listed at the bottom of this page.

Use your own words

Pretend you are an explorer in a new land. Write a letter home about the place where you decide to settle and start a city. Use a separate piece of paper and try to answer these questions in your letter:

- Where did you travel from?
- How did you get to your new place?
- What kind of place is it? Why did you choose it?
- What are the first things you will want to do here?
- What do you hope this place will be like in the future?

When students have finished their letters, give them an opportunity to draw a picture of their new city. Then invite volunteers to share their work with the class.

Find out more

Did you enjoy "How Does a City Grow?" If so, read more about how cities grow. Look for these books in your library:

- Finsand, Mary Jane. *The Town That Moved.* Carolrhoda, 1983.
- Gibbons, Gail. *Up Goes the Skyscraper.* Four Winds, 1986.
- Isadora, Rachel. *City Seen from A to Z.* Greenwillow, 1983.

2 Before reading *"Wildlife in the City"*

Think of what you know

You already know many things that help you when you read. Have you ever seen raccoons in a garbage can? What other wild animals can live in a city? Talk about your ideas. Then write what you think this story will be about.

This selection discusses the changing habitats of wild animals such as raccoons and opossums due to human encroachment. It then describes the successful adaptation of raccoons and opossums, and the dangers they face in a city. It closes by summarizing people's efforts to ensure the continued survival of urban wild animals. Discuss with students any wildlife they have seen in or near their neighborhoods. Ask them what these creatures eat, where they sleep, and how they protect themselves and their young.

Decide what you want to learn

Always read with questions in mind. Then you can look for answers to them. Look at the pictures on pages 46 and 47. What do they show?

The illustration on page 46 shows small woodland animals in a natural forest setting. The photograph on page 47 shows a fox foraging for food in an urban environment. Students may note that foxes appear in both pictures but that the settings are very different.

Write one thing you hope to learn from this story.

Students may want to know how wild animals can live in a city.

Get ready to use your reading skills

As you read, you need to put facts together. Sometimes a story does not tell you how all the facts fit. The questions in the green boxes will help you. They ask you to think about:

Where the facts lead. You already know some facts. Others are given in the story. Can you put them together to figure out new ideas?

How things are alike or different. Can you compare things, events, people, or ideas to understand more about them?

Why things happen. Can you figure out why something happens in the story? Can you see what happens because of it?

Understand the words

Here are some words from "Wildlife in the City." Use the story and pictures to help you understand them.

adapt	**opossum**	**survived**
nocturnal	**predators**	**wildlife**

To help students with new vocabulary write the word *wildlife* on the chalkboard and have students suggest related words. Add each of the new words to a web, asking students to explain how the words could refer to wildlife in a city. Encourage them to include as many aspects of animal life and habits as possible.

2 Reading

Wildlife in the City

Pretend you are standing in the middle of a big city. Night is just beginning to fall. Listen to the city's hum. Look around you at all the big buildings and busy streets. Can you imagine what the land looked like long ago, before there was a city? There was nothing then but a quiet forest full of animals. They could build their homes wherever they wished.

Think About It

▷ What do you think happened to the animals when people began to build a city where they lived?

Possible responses include: The animals moved to new locations, they died out, people killed them, they went to zoos, etc. Ask students to give reasons for their answers.

In this quiet forest, it is growing dark. A mother raccoon creeps down to a little stream. Raccoons have visited this same stream for hundreds of years. This one has come to find food. Her four babies wait in their nest inside a tree. The raccoon's strong, sharp claws turn over stones in the stream. Suddenly she grabs a big frog. She heads back to the tree with it in her mouth.

Here comes an animal that has lived in this forest since the time of the dinosaurs. It is the **opossum.** The opossum hunts for bugs, nuts, and anything else it can find. These animals have survived for so long because they can learn to live in a new way, or **adapt.** When the world around them changes, they change too. They learn to use whatever is around them for food and homes.

Now the forest is gone. But look quickly! You will see a mother raccoon stick her head out of an old pipe. This is where she has built her nest. There is no more forest stream where she can find frogs. But her tiny paws are good at pulling lids off garbage cans. Raccoons will eat almost anything they can find in the city. They are good at finding new homes in the city, too. Before the pipe, the mother raccoon lived inside an old car at the dump! What other wild animals still live here?

Think About It

▷ How has the raccoon adapted to life in the city?

To help students answer this question, have them compare how the raccoon finds its food and shelter in the wild and in the city. Help students understand that the different actions of the animal in the city show how it has adapted to city life. Adaptations include living in a pipe and an old car and eating from garbage cans.

A mother opossum is climbing down a light pole. Three babies are riding on her back. The family is on its way to the garbage cans. But the mother opossum will also visit the zoo tonight. She loves the nuts and other things she finds there. She has learned how to find food in the city. No wonder opossums have survived for so long on earth. They don't need one place for a home. They may sleep in a new place every night. They might sleep in an old box, a pipe, or under a porch.

In the forest the raccoon and the opossum faced danger from **predators.** Predators are animals that hunt, kill, and eat other animals. In the city, though, there are different dangers. Dogs, cars, and people are all dangers for wild animals. But raccoons and opossums have learned how to stay alive.

Think About It

▷ What do you think the saying, "playing 'possum," means?

Answers will vary. Students may suggest that when someone is pretending to be hurt or asleep, that person is "playing 'possum." Explain that the opossum's main defense mechanism against predators is its ability to lie absolutely still, as if already dead.

Before students answer the question below, encourage them to review what they've read about raccoons and opossums. Similarities: Both adapt well, are nocturnal, and face dangers. Differences: Raccoons wash their food; opossums carry their young and don't sleep in one place.

Think About It

▷ How are raccoons and opossums alike? How are they different?

Raccoons and opossums are **nocturnal.** This means that they hunt their food at night and sleep all day. Being out at night in the city is safer for them. It is easier to hide, and there are not as many people, dogs, and cars. Both these animals have learned to make use of any hiding place they can find.

The scientific name of the raccoon means "the washer." Raccoons like to put their food in water before they eat it. But city raccoons cannot always find fresh water. To make up for this, they might find a puddle on a sidewalk. Or a cat dish at someone's back door might give them the water they need.

Think About It

▷ How many wild animals are in the picture? How have they adapted?

Too many wild animals in a city can be a problem for the animals themselves. When these animals lived in the wild, predators kept their numbers down. There was enough food for all. But very few predators live in our cities. The number of wild animals sometimes grows too large. Then there is not enough food to go around.

The picture shows raccoons, a squirrel, opossums, and birds. Students may note the following signs of adaptation: The raccoon is opening a garbage can, the opossum is climbing down a telephone pole, the birds are sitting on telephone wires, the squirrel is running along the wires. Ask students to identify possible dangers for the animals in the picture as well (the man, the dog, the car, the wires).

Wild city animals must be ready to move at any time. A bulldozer may move onto an empty lot and clear away their homes. Foxes living in a pipe suddenly find themselves without a home when the city decides the old pipe must be moved. Most animals adapt to these troubles. But what about the ones who cannot? What about the baby foxes who have lost their mother?

Answers for the question below will vary. Students may differ on whether caring for wild animals is something a city should do. Make sure students try to justify their opinions.

Think About It

▷ Study the daily log of the Wildlife Center. Do you think the center is important? Why or why not?

Many cities have wild animal centers to help with these problems. It is here where a city worker will bring the baby foxes he has found. It is here where a hurt or sick raccoon can get well. When the animals can once again make a life for themselves in the city, the center sets them free.

It is amazing that wild animals live at all in our cities. But they do, thanks to the changes they have made and a little help from city people.

City of Riverton Wildlife Center
Daily Log

DATE	ANIMAL	WHERE FOUND	PROBLEM
May 1	baby opossum	21st St.—gutter	attacked by dog
May 1	box turtle	crossing—19th Ave.	in danger from cars
May 1	grey squirrel	sidewalk—13th St. and 18th Ave.	sick, hungry
May 2	3 raccoon cubs	building site—airport	lost from mother

2 After reading *"Wildlife in the City"*

Think about the story

1. Why is it important for city wildlife to be able to adapt?

Answers will vary. Possible responses include: Animals that don't change their way of living may not survive. They may not be able to find food or shelter. If they don't learn to stay away from new dangers, such as dogs, cars, and people, they might be hurt or killed.

2. What do you think it would be like if there were no wildlife in our cities?

Answers will vary. Some students may suggest that cities would be better off without wild animals, since animals turn over garbage cans and may carry disease. Other students may note that city life wouldn't be as interesting without squirrels and other wild animals.

3. What wild animals live in your community? What could people do to make their lives easier?

Answers will vary. Possible responses include: People could try not to hurt the animals; they could leave places where animals live, such as old pipes, alone; they could support wild animal centers in their town or city; they could report sick or hurt animals to a local animal care facility. Encourage students to explain their suggestions.

4. Think about wild animals that live in the woods and wild animals that live in the city. Then fill in this chart. Show how life is different for them in these two places.

	Where They Find Food	Where They Find Homes	Dangers They Face
In the Woods	in streams, in trees, on the ground	in trees, in hollow logs, in holes in the ground, in caves	other wild animals, hunters
In the City	in garbage cans and dumps, in gardens, in pet food dishes	in old pipes, in abandoned cars or buildings, under porches or decks	dogs, cars, people, electric wires, lack of food

Check what you learned

Turn back to page 45. Read again what you wanted to learn from this story. Did you find out what you wanted to know? If so, tell what you learned.

Answers will vary depending on the goals students set for themselves.

Were all your questions answered? If not, tell how you could find the answers.

Students may mention finding answers to their questions in a library. If your community has a wild animal center or shelter, students also might invite an animal care worker to visit class. In addition, suggest that students read more about wildlife in the books listed at the bottom of this page.

Use your own words

Pretend you are a wild animal that suddenly finds itself in the middle of a city. You have always lived in the forest. Use a separate sheet of paper to write about what you would do to survive. Try to answer these questions:

- How would you find food and water?
- How would you find a home?
- How would you stay safe from the dangers of the city?

You may want students to follow the steps of the writing process described on page T10 of this Annotated Teacher's Edition to complete their writing. When students have finished, have them take turns reading aloud their animal survival stories.

Find out more

Did you enjoy "Wildlife in the City"? If so, read more about wildlife. Look for these books in your library:

- Curtis, Patricia. *All Wild Creatures Welcome.* Lodestar Books, 1989.
- Hess, Lilo. *The Curious Raccoons.* Scribners, 1968.
- Kohl, Judith and Herbert. *The View from the Oak.* Scribners/Sierra Club Books, 1977.

3 Before reading "A City's Bones"

Think of what you know

You already know many things that help you when you read. Look at the title of this story. What "bones" might a city have? Talk about your ideas. Then write what you think this story will be about.

This selection describes the fossils found in the La Brea Tar Pits in Los Angeles—how they got there, what preserved them, and how they were discovered. The selection also explains how the pits were formed and how they were used by the early Native American and Mexican communities. Ask students what kinds of objects they might find buried underground and why some things might last longer than others. Then lead a class discussion about fossils.

Decide what you want to learn

Always read with questions in mind. Then you can look for answers to them. Study the picture on page 54. What do you think it shows?

The illustration shows prehistoric animals getting stuck in the tar.

Write one thing you hope to learn from this story.

Students might want to know where bones of animals like the ones in the picture could be found in a city.

Get ready to use your reading skills

As you read, you need to put facts together. Sometimes a story does not tell you how all the facts fit. The questions in the green boxes will help you. They ask you to think about:

What people are feeling. Can you put yourself in another person's place? Can you imagine what that person feels or thinks?

Where the facts lead. You already know some facts. Others are given in the story. Can you put them together to figure out new ideas?

What happens next. Can you use your own thinking and story clues to tell what will happen next?

Understand the words

Here are some words from "A City's Bones." Use the story and pictures to help you understand them.

buffalo	**mammoths**	**saber-toothed**
fossils	**museum**	**tar**
leak	**rotted**	**teratorns**

To help students with the new vocabulary, ask them to think about how the words could be related. Then have students work with partners to write a story in which they use all of the words.

3 Reading

A City's Bones

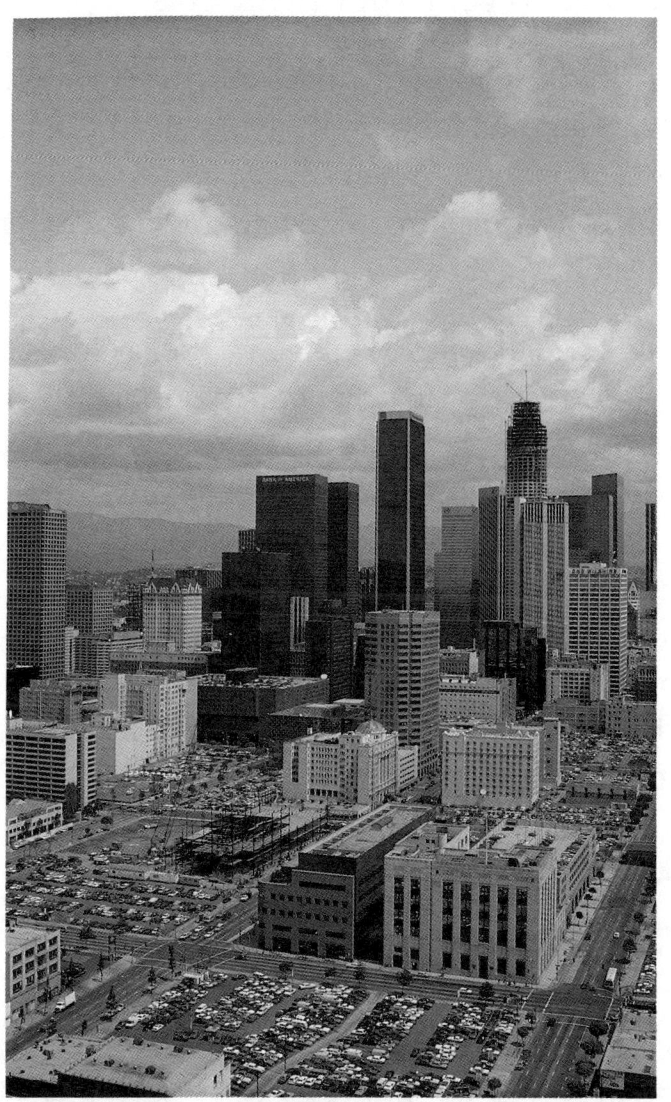

Los Angeles is the second largest city in the United States. Cars jam its fast roads and long streets. Tall buildings stand close together in its center. But in a park only minutes from downtown, there are bones. Old bones. Bones that have turned black.

The bones come from animals no living person has ever seen. Saber-toothed cats. Mammoths 13 feet tall. Giant birds called **teratorns,** whose wings stretched 14 feet.

These animals have not walked the earth for thousands of years. Their bones should have rotted long ago. Yet many are still found in the middle of a huge city. How could this happen? Why are the bones still whole? Why are so many found in one place?

Think About It

▷ What do you think the story will tell about these old bones?

If students have difficulty making a prediction, have them reread the third paragraph on this page. Guide students to predict that the selection will probably answer the questions in this paragraph.

To answer these questions you have to know about **tar.** Under Los Angeles are large fields of oil. Some of this oil comes up through cracks in the ground. It collects in pools. Over time, it gets drier and thicker. It forms tar.

Many tar pits formed near Los Angeles over the years. One group of pools is known as the La Brea Tar Pits. *La Brea* means "the tar" in Spanish. Animals and people lived near the La Brea Tar Pits for thousands and thousands of years.

People have used the tar pits in many ways. Around 1800, a ranch stood near the La Brea Tar Pits. It was called Rancho La Brea. At that time, Los Angeles was a part of Mexico. Mexican settlers used to come to Rancho La Brea to get tar for their roofs.

For hundreds of years before that, Native Americans came to the La Brea pits. They used the tar to seal their straw baskets. When the tar dried, nothing could leak out of the baskets. They also used the tar to fix broken tools.

But before people began to use it, La Brea belonged to the animals. Ten thousand years ago and more, there were huge herds of animals around Los Angeles. Every year the herds would come to the fields near La Brea. Often a buffalo or deer would not notice the tar pool. Leaves and grass hid the sticky tar. The animal would get stuck and die. Other animals, like bears or lions, would try to feed on the first animal. So would birds. Then they, too, would get stuck. Over time, all the bones would sink into the tar.

Answers to the question below will vary. Possible response: They probably liked having the tar pools nearby, since the tar could be useful. They were probably also a little afraid of the tar pools because people and animals could get caught in them.

Think About It

▷ How do you think Native Americans and Mexican settlers felt about tar pools?

Possible response to the question below: The tar pits would probably be protected because scientists would want to study the fossils found there. You may want to model how students could make that prediction based on the reaction of the scientists and what they read about the fossils and the park at the beginning of the selection.

Think About It

▷ What do you think will happen to the La Brea Tar Pits?

The tar was a trap. But it was more than that. The tar coated the bones of the animals. It turned them black. And it kept them safe. With a tar coating, the bones could not rot. They could last for thousands of years until someone found them. Very old bones like these are called **fossils.**

The early settlers of Los Angeles used to find bones in the tar. But they just threw them away. They had no idea the bones were fossils. By 1875, Major Henry Hancock owned Rancho La Brea. One day he found a huge, sharp tooth in the tar. It was eight inches long! He knew no living animal had a tooth like that. He sent the tooth to a scientist in Boston.

The scientist saw that the tooth belonged to a saber-toothed cat. These fierce animals had died out long ago. Other scientists began to look for fossils at the Hancock ranch. They found fossils that came from hundreds of different kinds of animals.

Scientists now understood how important the tar pits were. So did the Hancocks. In 1915, they gave part of Rancho La Brea to Los Angeles for a park. It was called Hancock Park. Years later, a man named George Page gave money to build a museum at Hancock Park just for the La Brea bones. The Page Museum of La Brea Discoveries opened in 1977.

For the first question below, remind students that meat eaters often went to the tar pits to feed on animals grazing nearby as well as those that had gotten stuck in the tar. Help them conclude that the frequency of meat eaters' visits would make it more likely for more of them to get stuck.

Since scientists first began to look in the pits for bones, there have been more than 100 digs at Rancho La Brea. Scientists have found thousands of bones. Most of them are from animals that lived 10,000 to 40,000 years ago. This was a time called the Ice Age. Much of Canada and the United States lay under huge sheets of ice. To scientists, the bones at Rancho La Brea are like a window into the Ice Age.

Ice Age: 40,000 years ago
Animals get stuck in the tar.

Ice Age ends: 10,000 years ago
Native Americans use tar to make tools.

1800
Mexicans use tar for roofs.

1875
Hancock finds tooth at his Rancho La Brea.

1915
Hancock gives land for Hancock Park.

1977
Page Museum opens.

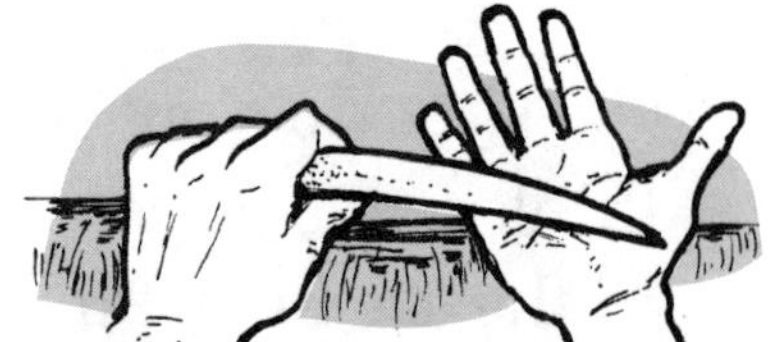

For the second question below, students may suggest that people knew the dangers of the tar pits and were careful to stay away from them. You may want to model using information from the selection (*The tar was a trap.*) and knowledge from real life (people avoid danger) to show how such a conclusion might be drawn.

Think About It

▷ Why do you think more meat eaters got stuck in the tar than other animals?

▷ Humans are also meat eaters. Why do you think more humans did not get stuck in the tar?

So far, the bones of over 420 different kinds of animals have been found at La Brea. Most came from meat eaters, like coyotes, saber-toothed cats, and giant bears. But there are also bones from birds, lizards, snakes, turtles, toads, frogs, and fish. The remains of snails, insects, and seeds have been found as well.

There is even one set of human bones. They belonged to a young Native American woman who lived nearly 9,000 years ago. She was about 4 feet 10 inches tall. No one knows how she got into the tar. She is the only human ever found there.

Los Angeles today has all the marks of a great city. It has new museums, fast roads, and tall buildings. It also has a past living in tar. Many people go to the Page Museum to see that past. And people who live near Hancock Park still dig in their gardens. Often they find tar. Sometimes, they find bones. They find not just a city's bones. They find the Ice Age.

3 After reading *"A City's Bones"*

Think about the story

1. The story tells how we opened a window into the Ice Age. Look back and put the steps below in order. Write the numbers *1* to *4* on the lines to show the order.

   __2__ Ice Age animals get stuck in the tar.

   __1__ Oil comes up to form tar pools.

   __4__ Scientists study the bones.

   __3__ The tar coats the bones and keeps them from rotting.

2. Suppose you found a strange bone. Would you know what it was from? How could you find out?

Answers will vary. Some students may say that they would have a better chance of recognizing a bone from a common, modern-day animal, such as a cow. Others may say they would have no idea what it was. They could find out by asking a biologist or an expert at a museum, or by comparing the bone with pictures in a book.

3. No one has ever seen a saber-tooth tiger or a teratorn. How do you think scientists can figure out what these animals looked like?

Scientists can figure out what these animals looked like based on the size and structure of their bones, and by studying the modern animals these animals have evolved into. Students might also recognize that the prehistoric animal models in museums are also helped by scientists' imaginations—scientists sometimes have to guess, too.

4. Many of the fossils from Rancho La Brea are seeds and plants. What might this tell scientists about the Ice Age at La Brea?

Fossils from seeds and plants help give scientists an idea of what kinds of plants lived in the area long ago. Guide students to see that a knowledge of plant life could also help scientists study what the weather and climate was like long ago.

Check what you learned

Turn back to page 52. Read again what you wanted to learn from this story. Did you find out what you wanted to know? If so, tell what you learned.

Answers will vary depending on the goals students set for themselves.

Were all your questions answered? If not, tell how you could find the answers.

Students may mention going to the library or a natural history museum to find answers to their questions. Also, suggest that students discover more about fossils and prehistoric animals by reading the books listed at the bottom of this page.

Use your own words

With a time machine, you could travel to any time in history. Go back to the Ice Age and visit the tar pools at La Brea. Write a report for the 1990s about what you find there. Use a separate piece of paper and try to answer these questions:

- What do the tar pools look like?
- What animals come near the pools?
- What happens to the animals?
- What do you do to keep from getting stuck in the tar?

Give students an opportunity to illustrate their reports. Then call on volunteers to present their reports to the class. You might also combine all the reports and illustrations into a class book, "Life in the Ice Age." Display the book in the class reading center.

Find out more

Did you enjoy "A City's Bones"? If so, read more about fossils. Look for these books in your library:

- Arnold, Caroline. *Trapped in Tar: Fossils from the Ice Age.* Clarion Books, 1987.
- Robinson, William W. *Beasts of the Tar Pits: Tales of Ancient America.* Ward Ritchie Press, 1961.

4 Before reading *"Plugging into Power"*

Think of what you know

You already know many things that help you when you read. What things do you plug in? What happens then? Why don't they work when you pull out the plug? Talk about your ideas. Then write what you think this story will be about.

This selection begins by describing the effect of a power outage on Oakland, California. It goes on to relate various sources of electrical energy and the production of electricity from them. Included are fossil fuels and hydroelectric, wind, and geothermal power. The advantages and disadvantages of each energy source are discussed as well. The selection ends by emphasizing the importance of energy conservation. Have students discuss the role of electricity in their daily lives and imagine what life might be like without it. Invite them to share what they know about the sources of electricity.

Decide what you want to learn

Always read with questions in mind. Then you can look for answers to them. Look at the picture on page 61. What do you think is happening there?

The illustration is a simple diagram of the production of electricity from natural gas.

Write one thing you hope to learn from this story.

Students may want to know how electricity is produced and how it gets to their homes.

Get ready to use your reading skills

As you read, you need to put facts together. Sometimes a story does not tell you how all the facts fit. The questions in the green boxes will help you. They ask you to think about:

Where the facts lead. You already know some facts. Others are given in the story. Can you put them together to figure out new ideas?

Why things happen. Can you figure out why something happens in the story? Can you see what happens because of it?

Understand the words

Here are some words from "Plugging Into Power." Use the story and pictures to help you understand them.

air conditioners **electricity** **energy** **fossil fuels** **generators** **heaters** **natural gas** **turbines** **windmills**

To help students with new vocabulary, have them fill in an **Energy** chart. Write two headings on the chalkboard: THINGS THAT MAKE ENERGY and THINGS THAT USE ENERGY. Have students discuss the new vocabulary terms and list them under the appropriate headings to complete the chart.

4 Reading

Plugging into Power

Suddenly the lights go out. The city grows dark and quiet. In homes, radios and TVs go off. Kitchen machines stop running. Outside, cars slow down. The streets are dark, and traffic lights aren't working. Without electricity, life seems to come to a stop.

Soon, though, the lights go back on. Workers from the power company found the problem. A power line blew down in a strong wind. The workers put it back up. Electricity again flows into the city of Oakland.

For the questions in the first box below: A strong wind blew a power line down, causing the electricity to stop flowing and the lights to go out. Once the line was fixed, the electricity began to flow and the lights went back on. You may want to illustrate this cause-effect chain on the chalkboard, using arrows to show the relationship of events.

Think About It

▷ What caused the lights to go out? What caused them to go on again?

Electricity is one kind of **energy.** Energy is power that can do work. Cities need a lot of energy for homes and factories. Much of it comes to people as electricity. But where does electricity come from?

Nature makes some kinds of electricity. Lightning is electricity. Some eels make electricity in their bodies to kill other fish. But we haven't found ways to use any of nature's electricity. We have to make our own.

Think About It

▷ Where do you think the heat that the generators use comes from?

Electricity is made by machines called **generators.** Generators use heat to turn water into steam. Then the steam spins huge wheels called **turbines.** And these spinning turbines make electricity. The electricity runs through wires to people's homes and places of work.

Encourage students to speculate about this question by thinking of different natural sources of heat. They might suggest volcanoes, hot springs, the sun, or fire. Explain that as they read they will learn about different ways people make heat to turn turbines and create electricity.

Generators need lots of heat to make electricity. Most power plants make heat by burning oil or natural gas or coal. These are **fossil fuels.** Fossil fuels come from animals that died long, long ago. A little fossil fuel makes enough electricity for hundreds of homes.

Cities like Oakland don't just have hundreds of homes, though. They have hundreds of thousands of homes, and thousands of offices and factories. Each one needs electricity. So the power company uses large amounts of fossil fuels. We also use fossil fuels in cars and buses. And we make them into plastic and cloth. No wonder we are running out of fossil fuels!

Think About It

▷ Do you think it is important to use other kinds of energy than fossil fuels? Why or why not?

Model using information from the selection (*we are running out of fossil fuels*) and real-life knowledge (when people start running out of something, they need to look for something else to replace it) to draw the conclusion that it is very important to look for new energy sources.

To the east of Oakland there are two kinds of fossil fuels in the earth. Natural gas lies under the ground near the Sacramento River. Coal is under nearby hills. The power company burns some of the natural gas to make electricity for Oakland and the rest of the Bay Area. But the coal stays in the ground.

Why does the power company use one fuel and not the other? One good thing about natural gas is that it burns cleanly. It does not add much dirt to the air. Coal does not burn cleanly. It makes a lot of smoke when it burns. There are special machines that make coal smoke cleaner. But these machines cost a lot of money. So using natural gas to make electricity is a good choice. It costs less to keep the air clean.

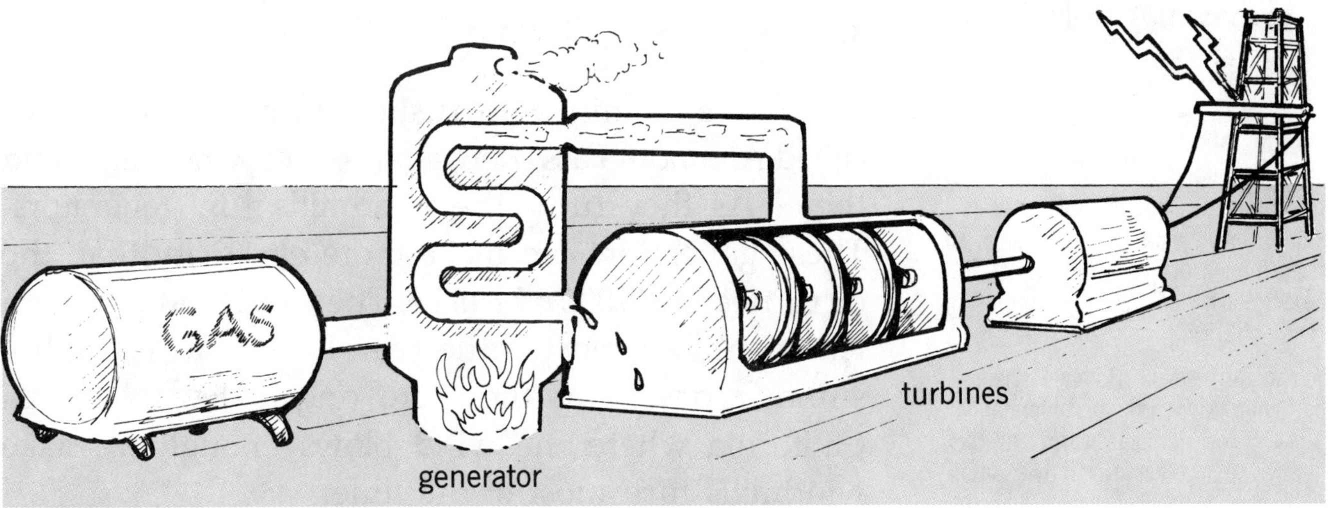

Possible response to the question below: The rivers and streams are dammed, and the water that is let out pushes turbines to create electricity.

Think About It

▷ How do rivers and streams help fill the Bay Area's energy needs?

Not all of Oakland's electricity comes from fossil fuels. Some comes from mountain rivers. The rivers are held back by dams. Only a little water is let out at a time. This water pushes turbines as it rushes down toward the sea. The electricity it makes goes to homes and factories in Oakland and many other cities. It also goes to farms in the big Sacramento Valley.

Water power doesn't make the air dirty. It doesn't use fuel that we could run out of. Rivers fill up every year when rain falls and snow melts. The huge dams cost a lot of money, though. And they also change the land by flooding river valleys.

Think About It

▷ How could you prove that hot air rises?

Thinking about this question will help students understand how wind forms in the Altamont Pass. Possible answers include: Smoke from a fire goes up, steam rises from a pot of boiling water, the heat from a heater vent comes up instead of staying near the floor.

You might also do a simple science experiment to confirm this information. Allow a desk lamp to warm and then gently tap together over it two cotton balls that have been lightly dipped in powder. Students will be able to observe the powder particles rising on the currents of the warmed air.

All through the summer the Sacramento Valley is very, very hot. The air over the ocean to the west is much cooler. This difference makes the air move. The hot air in the valley rises. The cool ocean air rushes east over some low mountains to take its place. That moving air is what we call **wind.**

Some of this wind rushes through a low place called Altamont Pass. Row after row of windmills stand there. As they turn, the windmills run generators. These generators can make more electricity than the oil carried by 25,000 oil trucks. The wind blows through Altamont Pass most of the year. It is strongest on hot summer days. But there are only a few places in California where the wind blows enough to make windmills turn most of the time.

Possible response to the question below: To get to the steam, workers must drill deep down into the earth. They have to keep drilling in different places until they find a spot in the earth where a great deal of steam is being produced. You might also ask students to speculate on the kind of equipment needed for such an operation and lead them to conclude that it costs a great deal of money, too.

Think About It

▷ Why does it cost so much money to try to get more steam power?

Just north of the Bay Area, people are digging deep inside the earth. They aren't looking for oil or gold. They want hot water. In some places, there is hot water deep under the ground. When the diggers reach this hot water, the water comes up as steam. And this steam can turn turbines to make electricity.

One out of every ten homes in the Bay Area gets its electricity from this steam power. But no one knows how to get more without spending a lot of money.

People in Oakland and the other cities in the Bay Area have many ways to get electricity. Each of these ways brings some problems, though. Like many others, people in Oakland are learning ways to use less energy. They save electricity by turning off extra lights. They save by turning down their heaters and air conditioners.

Think About It

▷ Look at the pictures. What are the people doing to save energy?

When people use less power, less electricity needs to be made. Less fuel is burned. Fewer dams must be built. All these things save money. The air and water are cleaner. And there will be more energy for lights, TVs, and radios in years to come.

By turning off extra lights, people save electricity; by wearing an extra sweater instead of turning on the heat, they save energy, too; by riding a bike or walking instead of driving, people save gas.

4 After reading *"Plugging into Power"*

Think about the story

1. You have read about different kinds of power. Each one has some good things about it as well as some problems. Fill in the chart below to show the good things and the problems with each kind of power.

	What's Good About It	Problems
Coal	in large supply; does not cost much money	does not burn cleanly; makes harmful smoke; costs a lot to make the smoke cleaner
Natural gas	burns cleanly	limited supply; costs more than coal
Wind power	clean; not very expensive	only a few places with enough wind
Water power	clean; each year rain fills rivers again	expensive to build dams; floods river valleys; keeps fish from returning to lay eggs

2. Do you think it is important for scientists to try to find new ways of making electricity? Why or why not?

Answers will vary. Make sure that students can justify their opinions.

3. What can you do to save energy?

At home:

Answers will vary. Encourage students to demonstrate their understanding of the various ways electricity is used both at home and at school, as well as various strategies for conserving it.

At school:

Check what you learned

Turn back to page 59. Read again what you wanted to learn from this story. Did you find out what you wanted to know? If so, tell what you learned.

Answers will vary depending on the goals students set for themselves.

Were all your questions answered? If not, tell how you could find the answers.

Students might suggest going to the library to find answers to their questions. Suggest that they look for one or more of the books listed at the bottom of this page. If there is a power plant near your community, you might want to arrange a class visit to the facility.

Use your own words

Pretend you are the wind, the sun, or a big river. Write a story about how your energy is used by a power plant. Use a separate piece of paper for your story and try to answer these questions:

- What is it like to be the sun, the wind, or a river?
- How is your energy "caught" by the power plant?
- Where does the electricity you make go?
- How does this electricity help people?

You may want students to follow the steps of the writing process described on page T10 of this Annotated Teacher's Edition to complete their writing. When students have finished, invite them to take turns reading their stories aloud to the class.

Find out more

Did you enjoy "Plugging into Power"? If so, read more about energy. Look for these books in your library:

- Hendershot, Judith. *In Coal Country.* Alfred A. Knopf/Borzoi Books, 1987.
- Macaulay, David. *The Way Things Work.* Houghton Mifflin, 1988.
- Math, Irwin. *More Wires and Watts: Undertanding and Using Electricity.* Charles Scribner's Sons, 1988.

After reading *LIVING IN CITIES*

Think about what you've learned

Read each question. Fill in the circle next to the best answer.

1. What does a city need in order to grow?
   - Ⓐ tar pits
   - Ⓑ oil and steam
   - Ⓒ a nearby ocean
   - Ⓓ people and resources

2. How are water and wind used to help the people of the Bay Area?
   - Ⓐ They make electricity.
   - Ⓑ They clean the air.
   - Ⓒ They save animals.
   - Ⓓ They make oil.

3. What do wild animals need to do to survive in a city?
   - Ⓐ sleep in trees
   - Ⓑ adapt, or change
   - Ⓒ become predators
   - Ⓓ wash their food

4. The La Brea Tar Pits help us learn about
   - Ⓐ explorers of long ago.
   - Ⓑ the future of Los Angeles.
   - Ⓒ animals of long ago.
   - Ⓓ how a city grows.

Read each question. Write your answer on the lines.

5. You read about St. Augustine, Chicago, Los Angeles, and Oakland. Write two ways these cities are alike.

Answers will vary. Possible responses include: All four cities are close to natural resources; they all have good location; they all have homes, offices, factories, shops, parks, and places to learn about the city's history; they all have people who want to live there; they all have people who work together to make the city a good place to live.

6. Which city would you like to live in the most? Tell why.

Answers will vary. Encourage students to explain their choices.

Write about what you've learned

Plan the perfect city. Use another piece of paper and think about these important ideas as you make your plan:

location energy resources

If students have difficulty beginning their plan, suggest that they look again at the map on page 37 and the changes (if any) they made to it. Encourage students to use that map for inspiration in planning their perfect city. When students have finished their plans, arrange a wall display of their work.

UNIT **Three**

FARM AND RANCH LIFE

To start:
County fairs are usually held in late summer or early fall. Contests determine the best animals and crops raised during the past year, as well as foods made from the crops such as jams, jellies, pies, etc. New farm machinery and equipment is exhibited. There are also entertainment, including carnival games and rides, and lots of food.

Members of 4-H or Future Farmers of America exhibit their agricultural projects or livestock they raised. Sometimes the livestock is auctioned off so the young people can earn money to keep raising animals. Ask students if they've ever been to a fair. Have them share their experiences with the class.

A huge orange pumpkin is carefully lifted onto the scale. People can't believe their eyes. The scale reads 650 pounds! And here's a lemon that weighs five pounds. And there's a green bean more than a foot long. What is the farmers' secret for growing these giant vegetables?

In the next building, a young girl stands beside the pig she raised. She looks down at her red ribbon. Second place. Smiling happily, she thinks ahead. With the money she'll get for this pig, she'll be able to raise another. And next year at the fair, maybe she can win the blue ribbon!

All year, farmers and ranchers work hard. Farmers must keep their crops safe from bugs and bad weather. Ranchers have to take good care of their animals. Now, at the county fair, it's time for them to show off a little.

You already know something about living on farms and ranches

Think. Write some words that tell about living on a farm or ranch.

Answers will vary. Possibilities include: corn, cattle, tractor, hay, barn, goats, chickens, trees, etc.

Talk. Share your ideas. Talk with a few classmates. See who can answer these questions:

- What are some crops grown on farms?
- What kinds of animals are raised on ranches?
- What problems do farmers and ranchers sometimes face?

Answers will vary. Students may mention corn, alfalfa, wheat, vegetables, cattle, sheep, and problems such as bad weather, insect damage, etc.

Write. Think of two ways living on a ranch or farm would be like living in a city. Think of two ways it would be different. Write your ideas on another piece of paper.

When students have completed their writing, draw two columns on the chalkboard, one labeled **CITY** and the other **FARM/RANCH.** Have students share the similarities and differences they thought of as you list their points of comparison appropriately on the board.

New words, new uses

Some of the words in this unit may be new to you. Keep them in mind as you read the stories to come.

> **cattle:** cows, bulls, and steers
> **crops:** plants grown for food or other uses
> **insects:** small animals with six legs and no backbone, like flies, bees, and beetles
> **prairie:** wide, flat land with few trees

Predicting

Here are the names of the stories in Unit Three. Read them and look at the picture below. Then write three things you think you might learn from the stories.

Bird Heroes *Cow Town*
The Story of Dirt *Good Bugs, Bad Bugs*

Students will learn about: (1) the Mormons' move west, and how sea gulls saved the first wheat crop; (2) how animals and people use dirt, and the composition of soil; (3) the cow towns of the Old West and an African American cowboy, Nat Love; and (4) the role of beneficial insects in controlling pests that threaten crops.

New information

After you have finished this unit, you will know the answers to these questions and more:

- How did a group of birds save a community?
- What is dirt? Who needs it?
- What were cow towns? What happened to them?
- How do insects hurt and help farmers?

Ask students to examine the illustration above and then discuss the various components of farm life they see in it.

1 Before reading *"Bird Heroes"*

Think of what you know

You already know many things that help you when you read. How and why did people cross the United States 150 years ago? What do you know about the people who started farms in the West? Talk about your ideas. Then write what you think this story will be about.

This selection traces the history of the Mormon people through their settlement in the valley of the Great Salt Lake. It details the Mormons' efforts to make the barren land arable and describes their despair as they watched swarms of crickets attack their first wheat crop. The selection concludes with the saving of the crop by flocks of sea gulls—still honored citizens in the state of Utah. Have students share what they know about the settling of the American West, including some of the difficulties of travel and pioneer life. You might discuss how moving to a new place was different in the 1800s than it is now, and what people might have had to do in order to build a new community.

Decide what you want to learn

Always read with questions in mind. Then you can look for answers to them. Look at the picture on page 72. What is happening?

The picture shows men, women, and children fighting off large insects.

Write one thing you hope to learn from this story.

Students may want to know how birds could become heroes to settlers in the American West.

Get ready to use your reading skills

As you read, you need to put facts together. Sometimes a story does not tell you how all the facts fit. The questions in the green boxes will help you. They ask you to think about:

What happens next. Can you use your own thinking and story clues to tell what will happen next?

What people are feeling. Can you put yourself in another person's place? Can you imagine what that person feels or thinks?

Why things happen. Can you figure out why something happens in a story? Can you see what happens because of it?

Understand the words

Here are some words from "Bird Heroes." Use the story and pictures to help you understand them.

acres	**canals**	**monument**	**swarms**
antennae	**citizens**	**spat**	**thistle**

To help students with new vocabulary, read each word aloud and discuss its meaning. Challenge students to use the new words in sentences describing a pioneer town.

1 Reading

Bird Heroes

In the early 1800s, a young man named Joseph Smith started the Church of the Latter-day Saints. Its members were also called **Mormons.** The early Mormons did not have an easy time of it. Trouble always seemed to follow them.

Answers will vary for the question below. Students may note that people sometimes react violently to people they consider different from themselves. You might use this question as a lead-in to a general discussion of the roots of prejudice.

Think About It

▷ Why didn't people want the Mormons to live near them?

Wherever the Mormons settled, they had problems with their neighbors. The Mormons' ways of living and believing were different from other people. So the Mormons kept moving. But it was always the same. In Illinois they started a town that grew quickly into a city. Then again their neighbors tried to make them move away by burning their homes and farms. At times, people even shot at them. After one fight, Joseph Smith was killed.

The new leader was Brigham Young. He decided to go west. The Mormons left Illinois in February of 1846 for California.

Think About It

▷ Look at the map of the Mormon Trail. What do you think the trip west was like?

More than 15,000 Mormons made the long trip by mule, by horse, by covered wagon, and on foot. Sometimes they wondered if they would ever reach California. Many people got sick along the way. Some died. The people grew tired and sad. To cheer themselves up, they sang and told stories.

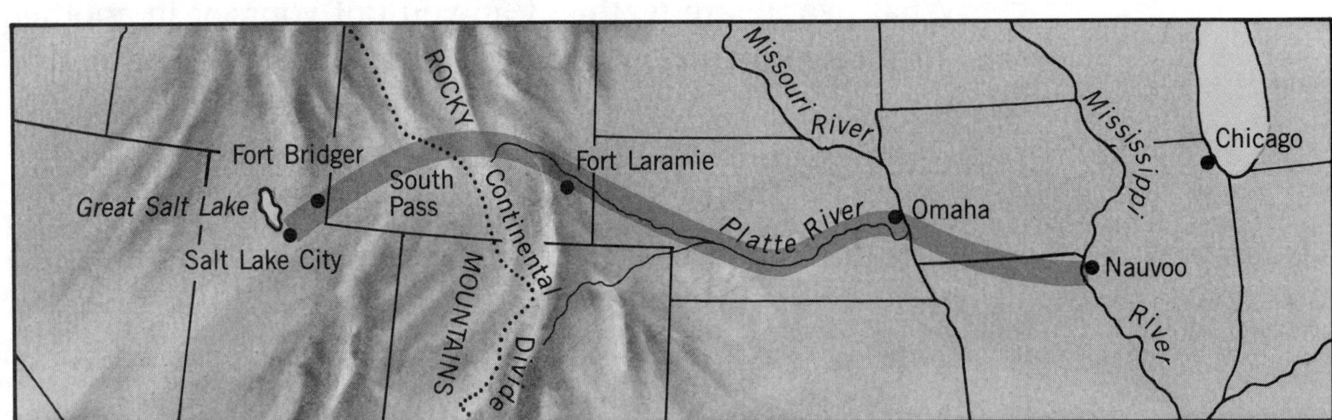

The trip was long and hard. The trail crossed deserts, mountains, and rivers. Food and water were sometimes hard to come by, and there was little medical care available. Travelers were also in danger of being attacked by outlaws or wild animals. Wagons of the sort the Mormons traveled in might cover 20 miles or less a day and often broke down.

On July 24, 1847, the Mormons came to the big Great Salt Lake valley. There was hardly a tree in sight. The valley was empty and dry. But Brigham Young surprised everyone. "This is the place!" he told them. "The Mormons will settle where no one else will settle. This way we will have no neighbors to bother us."

Think About It

▷ Imagine you are a Mormon child in 1847. You are hungry, hot, and tired of walking. You look out over a dry, empty valley with no trees. Your parents tell you this is your new home. How do you feel?

The Mormons met with many problems, but they did not give up. Instead, they got busy. Every man, woman, and child went to work. They cleared, plowed, and fenced 5,000 acres of dry soil. They dammed mountain streams, made water canals, and flooded the plowed land. Soon, the Mormons had rich farmland. But they didn't stop there. In the fall, they began to plant their fields. About 1,000 acres were planted with winter wheat.

Most students will probably say they would feel disappointed or upset, especially since they thought they were going to live in California, where conditions were better. Help students see how putting themselves in another person's place can help them understand that person's feelings.

That first winter was hard. It was very, very cold. There was little food to eat. The settlers got so hungry that they ate thistle tops and roots. Some people got sick from the food. Some of the smaller children died.

It was a sad time. But the Mormons remembered something they had learned on the trail. They remembered how to cheer themselves up. They met at night to sing and tell stories. It helped them pass the long winter nights.

Spring finally came. The winter wheat was just starting to come up. Now more acres could be planted. The Mormons began to think the worst was over. The year 1848 was going to be a good one.

Soon it was summer. The crops were doing well. It was almost time to harvest the wheat. Then one day, the people saw a strange sight in the hills. The hills had turned black. They seemed to be moving. Huge insects—as big as baby mice—began to sweep down from the hills! They had long antennae and strong back legs. The Mormons thought they were crickets. The crickets were everywhere, even inside houses. You couldn't walk anywhere without stepping on them!

For the questions below, answers will vary. Students will probably say no, a cricket by itself is not scary, but millions of them in an eating frenzy can be very scary. Possible causes include a disruption of their normal life and feeding cycles, etc.

Think About It

▷ Are crickets usually things to be afraid of? What do you think caused this to happen?

First, the insects attacked the fruit trees. Boys with sticks tried to protect the trees. But more and more came. Swarms of crickets covered the land like a blanket. The Mormons watched sadly as the insects hopped and crawled over the wheat crop. Now the fields were black. The Mormons tried to beat the crickets off with anything they could find. But it was no use. There were too many of them!

The people's dreams had become a nightmare. It was like the old days when neighbors had tried to burn them out. The Mormons had begun to make a good life for themselves again. Now that good life was being eaten away by bugs!

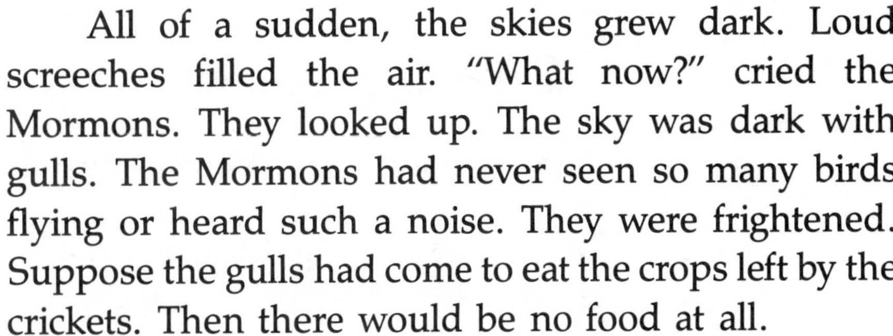

All of a sudden, the skies grew dark. Loud screeches filled the air. "What now?" cried the Mormons. They looked up. The sky was dark with gulls. The Mormons had never seen so many birds flying or heard such a noise. They were frightened. Suppose the gulls had come to eat the crops left by the crickets. Then there would be no food at all.

Think About It

▷ Why do you think the gulls are there?

The Mormons were in for a surprise, though. The gulls didn't eat the wheat. They ate the crickets! They ate them by the hundreds. And when they couldn't hold any more in their mouths, they spat them out dead and ate some more. The gulls were saving the crops! Now the Mormons could stay in the valley. Now they would finally have a home.

Today, gulls are special citizens in the state of Utah. No one may kill a gull. There is even a tall monument to the birds in Salt Lake City. Girls and boys still like to hear the story of the crickets and the gulls. The Mormons will never forget how the gulls helped save their new home.

Some students may guess that the gulls are there because they want to eat the crickets. Others may suggest that the gulls just happened to be flying by. You might help students to see that they can predict that the gulls will help because of the title of the selection and because the gulls would probably not appear in the selection unless they played an important role. If students wonder if these were "sea gulls," explain that there are different kinds of gulls. Many live on or near large inland bodies of water, such as the Great Lakes and the Great Salt Lake.

1 After reading *"Bird Heroes"*

Think about the story

1. Look at the list below. Think about what happened first, next, and last. Write the numbers *1* to *5* next to the events on the list to show their order.

   __4__ The crickets ate the crops.

   __1__ The Mormons were driven away by their neighbors.

   __2__ Brigham Young told the Mormons they would settle in the Great Salt Lake valley.

   __5__ The gulls ate the crickets.

   __3__ The Mormons planted crops on their new lands.

2. Why do you think singing helped the Mormons get through hard times?

Answers will vary. Possibilities include: Singing might have helped by reminding the Mormons that they weren't alone. There were others there to share the work and problems. Singing probably also took the people's minds off their problems and let them think about happier things. You might wish to point out the importance of singing to the Mormons by playing a recording by the Mormon Tabernacle Choir.

3. Suppose the crickets had eaten all the crops. What do you think would have happened to the Mormons?

Possible answers include: The Mormons would have moved on to another place; they would have planted again, but this time in a way that would protect the crops from crickets; they would have died of hunger; they would have struggled to live off the land.

4. In your own words, tell why gulls are important to the Mormons of Salt Lake City.

Possible answers include: They are important because they helped the Mormons survive in their new home. Without the gulls' help, the Mormons may not have been able to stay in the region or found Salt Lake City.

Check what you learned

Turn back to page 69. Read again what you wanted to learn from this story. Did you find out what you wanted to know? If so, tell what you learned.

Answers will vary depending on the goals students set for themselves.

Were all your questions answered? If not, tell how you could find the answers.

Students may mention going to the library as a way to find answers to their questions. In addition, direct students' attention to the books listed at the bottom of this page.

Use your own words

Write a news report about the amazing story of the crickets and gulls. Make sure you include a headline. Use a separate piece of paper and try to answer these questions:

- **Where** and **when** did the event take place?
- **Who** was there?
- **What** happened first? Next? After that?
- **How** did the story end?

You may want students to follow the steps of the writing process described on page T10 of this Annotated Teacher's Edition to complete this activity. When students have finished, have them share their news reports with the class.

Find out more

Did you enjoy "Bird Heroes"? If so, read more about how America was settled. Look for these books in your library:

- Bellville, Cheryl Walsh. *Farming Today Yesterday's Way.* Carolrhoda, 1984.
- Fritz, Jean. *The Cabin Faced West.* Puffin Press, 1987.
- MacLachlan, Patricia. *Sarah, Plain and Tall.* Harper & Row, 1985.

2 Before reading *"The Story of Dirt"*

Think of what you know

You already know many things that help you when you read. You know what *dirt* is, don't you? But have you ever looked at it closely? Do you know what it *really* is? Talk about your ideas. Then write what you think this story will be about.

This selection focuses on soil and its importance to life. A description of an ant colony reveals the mutually beneficial relationship between living creatures and dirt. Prairie dog and farm communities also highlight this interdependence. The selection goes on to explain the composition of soil, with loam being the most desirable. Finally, the selection describes various soil management techniques to keep soil healthy and productive. Encourage students to share their knowledge about soil. Ask them what dirt is good for and what life for farmers, plants, and animals that live underground might be like without it.

Decide what you want to learn

Always read with questions in mind. Then you can look for answers to them. Look at the picture on page 77. What do you see in it?

Students will probably recognize the picture as an ant colony. They might also note the various tunnels and chambers of the colony.

Write one thing you hope to learn from this story.

Students may be curious to learn "just what's so special about plain old dirt."

Get ready to use your reading skills

As you read, you need to put facts together. Sometimes a story does not tell you how all the facts fit. The questions in the green boxes will help you. They ask you to think about:

How things are alike or different. Can you compare things, events, people, or ideas to understand more about them?

Where the facts lead. You already know some facts. Others are given in the story. Can you put them together to figure out new ideas?

Why people do things. Can you use what people say and do to figure out why they act the way they do?

Understand the words

Here are some words from "The Story of Dirt." Use the story and pictures to help you understand them.

bacteria	**healthy**	**minerals**	**sprout**
burrows	**loam**	**prairie**	**volcanoes**

To help students with new vocabulary, read the words aloud and have students repeat them. Then have pairs of students look the words up in a dictionary. Call on volunteers to discuss the meaning of each word and to predict what the word has to do with soil.

2 Reading

The Story of Dirt

It is spring on the prairie. The sun shines brightly, and the air is hot and dry. Nothing moves. The land seems empty of all but grass. But is it? Look closely at the small pile of dirt at your feet.

Pretend you could see into that dark dirt. Suddenly, you can see a city. It is a city unlike any you have ever visited. That is because it is an ant city.

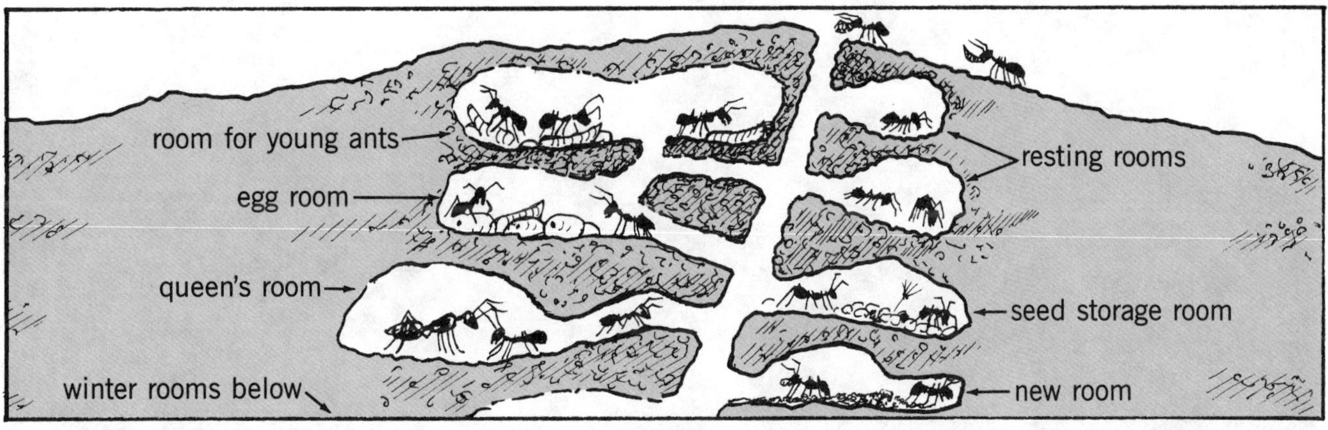

The ant city goes many feet under the ground. It has long, long tunnels and hundreds of tiny rooms. Thousands of ants live and work in it.

Answers for the question below will vary. Before students respond, you might have them consider the kinds of things people do in cities. Some similarities include: Both ants and people live in groups, they are busy, they work hard, they gather food, they take care of their young, and they add on to their cities and fix them when necessary.

Think About It

▷ How are the ants in this city like people in cities? How are they different?

You've never seen such a busy place! Ants are coming and going all the time. Some carry leaves and seeds to be eaten later. Others prepare the food. Some ants take care of the young. Others care for the queen that lays the eggs. Many ants work to build the city and keep it growing. They dig new rooms and fix tunnels. Worker ants carry dirt outside, one grain at time.

Ants need dirt. It is their home. But the dirt also needs ants. Ant tunnels let air and water into the ground. The ants' digging keeps the dirt from getting too hard. When ants die, their bodies mix with the dirt. This makes it richer and better for growing plants.

Nearby is another kind of city. It, too, is built under the ground. This one is a prairie dog town. Prairie dogs are a kind of ground squirrel. They dig **burrows,** or long holes, in the ground. These burrows keep them cool in the summer and warm in the winter. They can also get away from eagles or coyotes by hiding in their burrows. Prairie dog towns can grow very large. One town in Texas covered 25,000 square miles. It was home to about 400,000,000 prairie dogs!

Think About It

▷ What do you think might happen to the dirt if no ants, prairie dogs, or other animals lived in it?

Possible answers include: The dirt would become hard and plants would not grow well in it. The land might not be any good for farming, and that would mean less food for people to eat. You may want to model how students can put together facts from the story with what they already know to figure out new ideas.

Like ants, prairie dogs also help the soil. Their digging mixes the soil up and lets air and water in. This keeps the soil loose and healthy.

Not far away from the prairie dog town, the "people" town of Lakota is just waking. Ole Sundeen is a farmer. Today he has a quick breakfast and heads out to his fields. He is going to plant his crops.

Ole bends down to feel the dirt. It is soft and black. Last week he plowed the field. Now it is ready for seed. Ole smiles. In a few weeks the seeds will sprout. Soon, young wheat and corn plants will cover his land. Ole is thankful for the dirt under his feet.

Ants, prairie dogs, and farmers all need dirt. So does almost every other living thing. A few inches of soil cover just about all the land on earth. Plants grow in this soil. And from plants come food, wood for houses, clothes to wear, and even the air we breathe. But where does soil come from?

Mostly, soil comes from rock. Long, long ago, the earth was nothing but rock. Little by little, water broke the rock into smaller pieces. Rivers washed over the rock, and ice cracked it. Ocean waves pounded it. Only tiny pieces of rock were left to cover much of the land. In some places, volcanoes grew up. They threw out hot rocks and ash. These also covered the land.

Think About It

▷ How does water break down rock?

One way in which water breaks down rock is by flowing over it and gradually washing it away slowly and steadily for many, many years. If students have difficulty grasping this idea, you might point out how river rocks are rounded and polished by running water over the years. A picture of the Grand Canyon might also provide a dramatic and graphic display of how water can wear away rocks.

Over time, all these rocks were broken down into smaller and smaller pieces. But they still weren't dirt. Dirt needs to have living things in it. It needs tiny animals called **bacteria.** Bacteria first grew in the ocean. Then they came onto the land and mixed with rocks. This made dirt. Then plants could grow. Animals that feed on plants could grow, too.

Dirt is still being made all the time. Volcanoes pour ash on the land. Rock breaks into pieces. Animals and plants mix with these to make soil.

Soil is made up of different pieces of rock. The sand and clay in the rock have minerals in them that plants use as food. So the best soil for plants has the best mix of rock pieces in it. This soil is called **loam.** Loam is wet and black. It has lots of minerals and living things in it, like bacteria, worms, and bugs.

For the question below, soil is made up of rock pieces, including rock and ash from volcanoes. It also contains living things such as bacteria and dead plants and animals.

Think About It

▷ What are some of the things that make up soil?

Farmers like Ole Sundeen try to keep their soil healthy. They know that plants take their food from the soil. So they let some fields "rest" every other year. To give a field a rest, farmers don't plant crops in it. Or they might plant different crops in a field from year to year. They might plant corn one year and beans the next. The beans put minerals back into the soil that the corn has taken out.

Farmers also know that heavy rains or wind can carry soil away. It takes many years to make new soil. So farmers plant trees and other crops that hold the soil in place. They also plow in special ways so that rain water cannot wash the soil away.

Think About It

▷ Why do farmers work hard to keep the soil healthy?

Most of all, though, farmers try to keep their soil alive. They know that without living things in the soil, earth would just be pieces of rock.

Farmers work hard to keep their soil healthy because good soil is necessary to the success of their farming. Healthy soil produces a larger crop yield, while poor soil produces fewer and inferior crops.

2 After reading *"The Story of Dirt"*

Think about the story

1. What are two ways that ants help the soil?

By digging tunnels, ants allow air and water into the soil. Their digging also mixes the dirt and keeps it from getting too hard. When ants die, their bodies mix with the dirt and make it richer.

2. How is dirt like rock? How is it different?

Dirt is like rock because it contains many tiny rock pieces. It is different because it contains living things, like bacteria, which let plants grow in dirt. Plants cannot grow in solid rock.

3. Think about communities of ants, prairie dogs, and people. Name one way these communities are alike. Name the most important way they are different.

Possible answers include: They all need dirt to live, they are all alive, they work together, they live together in groups, and each member of the community has a job. Ants and prairie dogs live in the dirt; people use the dirt to grow things to eat.

4. List the things that are needed to make loam. Which do you think is the most important? Why do you think so?

Loam consists of different kinds of rock, which contain sand, clay, and many minerals, as well as living things such as bacteria, worms, and bugs. Encourage students to explain the reasons for their answers to the second part of the question. If necessary, help them to understand that each kind of rock has different minerals in it and holds water differently. If soil contained only one kind of rock, it would be too sandy, too muddy, or too thin for plants to grow.

Check what you learned

Turn back to page 76. Read again what you wanted to learn from this story. Did you find out what you wanted to know? If so, tell what you learned.

Answers will vary depending on the goals students set for themselves.

Were all your questions answered? If not, tell how you could find the answers.

Students may mention going to the library as a way to find answers to their questions. If possible, they might also visit a farm to find out more about dirt. In addition, encourage students to read the books listed at the bottom of this page.

Use your own words

Pretend you are an ant or a prairie dog. Write about a day in your life. Use a separate piece of paper and try to answer these questions:

- What is your home like?
- What do you do above the ground?
- What do you do below the ground?

Students may enjoy illustrating their stories about their day as an ant or prairie dog. When they are finished, invite students to share their writing with the class.

Find out more

Did you enjoy "The Story of Dirt"? If so, read more about dirt and soil. Look for these books in your library:

- McLaughlin, Molly. *Earthworms, Dirt, and Rotten Leaves.* Atheneum, 1986.
- Milne, Louis J. *A Shovelful of Earth.* Henry Holt, 1987.

3 Before reading *"Cow Town"*

Think of what you know

You already know many things that help you when you read. Have you ever seen a picture of a Wild West town? What do you know about the life of a cowboy in the Old West? Talk about your ideas. Then write what you think this story will be about.

This selection discusses the life of the cowboy, focusing on the African American cowboy, Nat Love. It describes cattle drives up the trails from Texas to the wild frontier cow towns where railroads took the cattle east to market. The selection ends with a look at modern African American rodeos in south Texas, where professional as well as "weekend" black cowboys still show off their roping and riding skills. Have students discuss cowboys and western life, including ranching and cattle drives, in the late 1800s. You might point out that cowboys, though often depicted as gunslingers, were really men who worked with cattle. (A number of women also worked with cattle on ranches during that period.)

Decide what you want to learn

Always read with questions in mind. Then you can look for answers to them. Look at the picture on page 84. What does it show?

The photograph is of Nat Love, a famous African American cowboy.

Write one thing you hope to learn from this story.

Students may want to know about the man in the picture and how he became a cowboy.

Get ready to use your reading skills

As you read, you need to put facts together. Sometimes a story does not tell you how all the facts fit. The questions in the green boxes will help you. They ask you to think about:

What people are feeling. Can you put yourself in another person's place? Can you imagine what that person feels or thinks?

Your own thoughts. Can your own thoughts help you judge what the story says?

Where the facts lead. You already know some facts. Others are given in the story. Can you put them together to figure out new ideas?

Understand the words

Here are some words from "Cow Town." Use the story and pictures to help you understand them.

adventures	**fistfights**	**rodeos**	**stampede**
cowhands	**outlaws**	**slavery**	**wrangler**

To help students with new vocabulary, create a semantic map for the word *cowboy* on the chalkboard. Encourage students to discuss each new word as it relates to cowboys and life in the Old West.

3 Reading

Cow Town

Nat Love looked out the window of the train as it pulled into the station. The year was 1869. Nat was just 15 years old. He had left his home in Tennessee weeks before. Now he had finally reached this town in western Kansas.

Think About It

▷ How do you think Nat felt when he first saw the town? Why?

▷ Why do you think these places were called "cow towns"?

But was this really it? Nat couldn't believe his eyes. The streets were filled with mud. The wooden buildings looked like they might fall down.

Then Nat saw something that made his eyes light up. Riding down the street was a group of cowboys. One of them was black, just like Nat. Nat smiled. Yes, this really was the famous cow town, Dodge City. If Nat was lucky, he would soon be a cowboy, too.

Dodge City was one of many cow towns that grew up in Kansas after the Civil War. These towns were built along new railroad lines. Cowboys would bring their cattle north from Texas on long cattle drives. When they reached the Kansas cow towns, the cattle would be loaded on trains and taken to cities in the East.

The Kansas cow towns were wild places. Dancing and drinking filled the nights with noise. And all the noise often led to fistfights and gun battles. But there was lots of money to be made here, too. For that reason, people from all over the country came to Dodge City. Some, like Nat Love, came to be cowboys.

Answers will vary. Students may suggest that Nat was disappointed because the town wasn't what he had expected. He might have felt foolish, too, since he had traveled so far to get there. If students have trouble imagining how he felt, help them recall times when they have looked forward to something and then been disappointed.

For the second question, ask students to explain the reasons for their answers.

Think About It

▷ What do you think life was like for the African American cowboys? Why do you think so?

Answers may vary. Students may say that life was hard, exciting, or dangerous. Some students may say that discrimination would have made life more difficult for African American cowboys. Explain that African Americans who were cowboys with proven skills often suffered less discrimination in the Old West than those in other jobs in other parts of the country.

Nat knew about black cowboys before he went to Kansas. In fact, by the late 1800s, one out of every five cowboys in the Old West was an African American. There were about 8,000 of them. Most black cowboys came from Texas. Before the Civil War, they had been slaves on Texas ranches. There they had learned to rope and ride and herd cattle. When slavery ended, many black cowboys stayed on to work for Texas ranchers as free men.

As a boy in Tennessee, Nat had also learned to ride horses. After a few days in Dodge City, he got a chance to prove himself to a Texas rancher. He got a job and rode off south to Texas.

Over the years, Nat had many adventures. He rode on cattle drives all over the West. He even went to Mexico.

One time, Nat was visiting the town of Deadwood, South Dakota. It was July 4, 1876. Lots of cowboys were in town for Independence Day. They held roping, riding, and shooting contests. Nat won them all. People called him the "Hero of Deadwood" and "Deadwood Dick." He became one of the most famous cowboys in all the West. He even wrote a book about his adventures.

The cattle drive was the biggest event in the life of a cowboy. Every year, teams of cowboys herded cattle up the trails from the Texas plains to cow towns in Kansas, Nebraska, Colorado, and Wyoming. There, they put the cattle on trains for the trip east. Usually it took 10 or 12 cowboys to run the cattle on a drive. There were a trail boss, a cook, and a wrangler, the man who took care of the horses. The rest were cowhands.

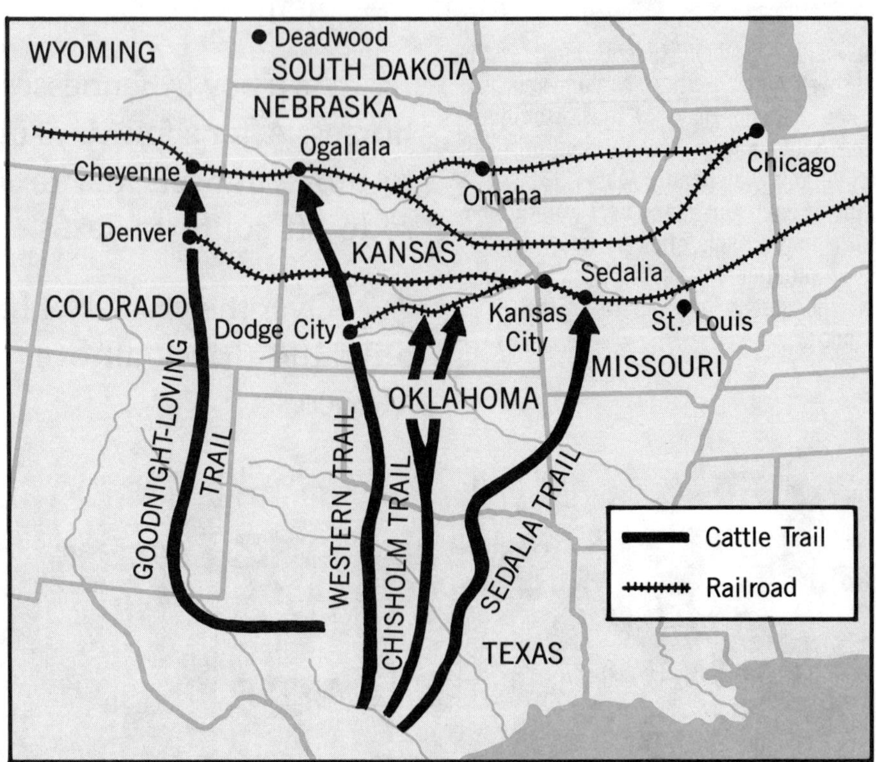

Think About It

▷ Cattle drives were often dangerous. What do you think some of the dangers could be?

Possible answers include: attacks by outlaws, bad weather, wild animals, stampeding cattle, falling off horses, flooding rivers, etc. Point out to students that cowboys worked in wild, lonely places without doctors or medical care nearby. An injury such as a broken bone or a bad cut might not be properly treated for days or weeks.

The cattle drive was long and hard. The cowboys had to make thousands of cattle walk over 1,000 miles. Sometimes the trip took two or three months. There were hot, dry lands and wide rivers to cross. Often there were sudden wild storms. Sometimes outlaws tried to take part of the herd. And sometimes the cattle might get frightened and **stampede.** They would run hard in all different directions. The cowboys might have to ride all day and all night just to round them up again.

Finally, the drive was over. The cowboys reached the Kansas cow towns. After cleaning up, they went into town to dance all night and spend their money. Then they rode home to Texas and back to work again.

Think About It

▷ Farming also helped to end the days of long cattle drives. Why do you think that was so?

Think About It

▷ Why do you think some people still want to be cowboys? Would you like to be a cowboy? Why or why not?

The days of the cattle drives are long gone. The wild cow towns are gone, too. Railroad lines go all over the country now. Cattle can be loaded on trains right near their home ranches.

There aren't many cowboys left now, either. But many of today's working cowboys can be found in Texas. And some of them are African Americans.

You can still see black cowboys at rodeos in south Texas. There are even rodeos where all the cowboys are black. And the roping and riding is just like in the old days. Some of these cowboys still work on ranches. But most live and work in cities. When the weekend comes, they put on their boots and hats. They become cowboys.

Today's African American cowboys may not ride the trails any more. But they keep alive the story of the black cowboy. And they help us remember the great cattle drives and cow towns of the past.

For the question in the first box, answers will vary. Cattle drives needed large areas of open land to drive the cattle through. When settlers began to farm, they built fences, which made cattle drives impossible. Without cattle drives, there was less need for cowboys. Encourage students to use what they already know to help them draw their conclusions.

For the questions in the second box, possible responses include: Some people still think the cowboy's life is exciting and fun because it includes riding horses and spending a lot of time outdoors. Make sure students provide reasons for their answers.

3 After reading *"Cow Town"*

Think about the story

1. Why do you think cow towns were such wild places?

Before students complete this activity, you might help them recall the circumstances of the cow towns: They were recently established, there was money to be made, and people came to them from all over the country. Also, life on the frontier was difficult, with few entertainments and fewer comforts. People were eager to have a good time and to make money from others, sometimes unfairly. Cowboys were temporary residents of these cow towns, so the locals might have been tempted to take advantage of them. Because the towns were new, there might be little law and order; disagreements often led to fighting.

2. Cowboys worked hard but were not paid much money. Why do you think Nat Love and so many others wanted to be cowboys?

Some people found the freedom and adventure of cowboy life exciting. Many also liked being outdoors and working with animals. You might model how students can use their own thinking to figure out ideas that are not explicitly stated in the selection.

3. Cowboys had to be good at many things. What were some skills you think they needed?

To complete this activity, lead students to think about the kinds of tasks cowboys had to carry out, and the conditions under which they worked. Possible answers include: riding horses, "breaking" horses, roping horses and cattle, branding, tying knots, helping injured animals, fixing gear, shooting, surviving in the wild, figuring out directions without a map, etc.

4. There were often problems on a cattle drive. What were some of those problems? Think about the story and what you already know to fill in the word web below. Answers will vary. Possibilities include:

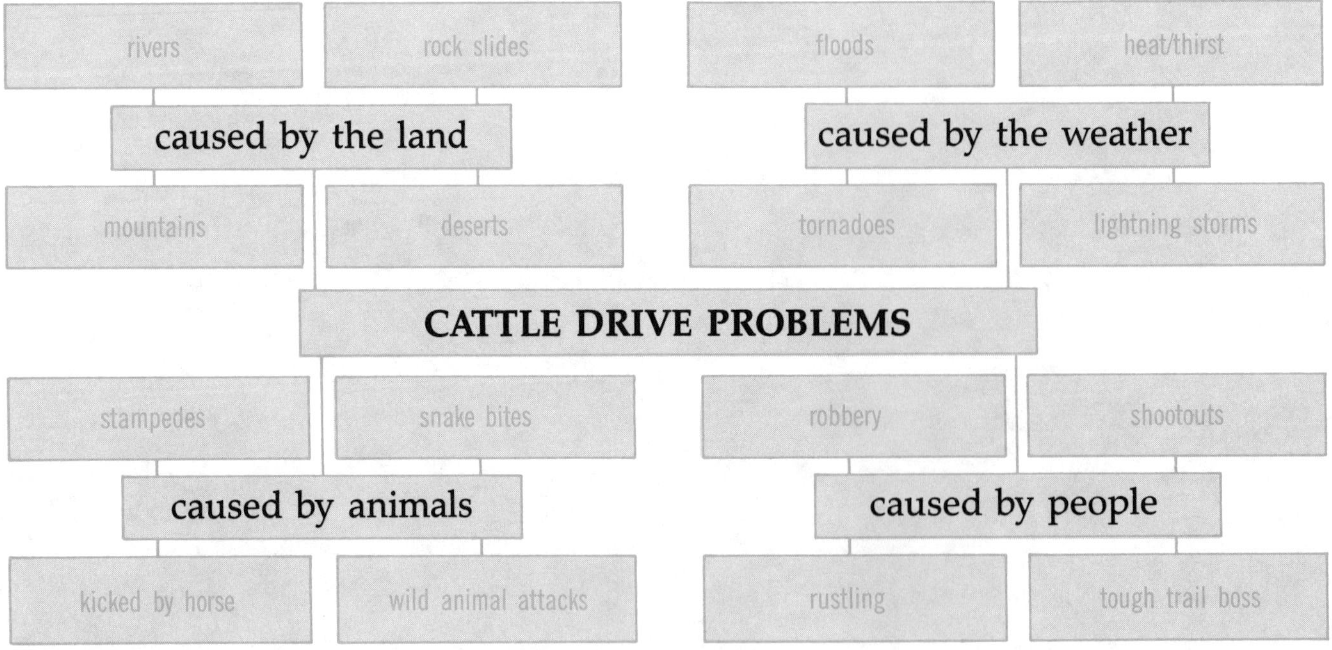

5. Today, people can still visit a working ranch near Houston, Texas, that is owned by African Americans. Would you like to visit it? Why or why not?

Answers will vary. Encourage students to explain why they would or would not like to visit this ranch.

Check what you learned

Turn back to page 83. Read again what you wanted to learn from this story. Did you find out what you wanted to know? If so, tell what you learned.

Answers will vary depending on the goals students set for themselves.

Were all your questions answered? If not, tell how you could find the answers.

Students may mention going to the library as a way to find answers to their questions. In addition, direct students' attention to the books suggested at the bottom of this page.

Use your own words

Pretend you are a cowboy riding on a cattle drive. Write about a day on the trail. Use a separate piece of paper and try to answer these questions:

- What kind of land are you riding through?
- What is your job on the drive?
- What special things happened on that day?
- How do you feel when you're on the trail?

You may want students to follow the steps of the writing process described on page T10 of this Annotated Teacher's Edition. Invite students to share their completed writing with the class. Students may also enjoy creating a bulletin board display about cowboys in the Old West.

Find out more

Did you enjoy "Cow Town"? If so, read more about cowboys in the Old West. Look for these books in your library:

- Freedman, Russell. *Cowboys of the Wild West.* Ticknor & Fields, 1985.
- Martini, Teri. *Cowboys.* Children's Press, 1981.
- McCall, Edith. *Cowboys & Cattle Drives.* Children's Press, 1980.

4 Before reading *"Good Bugs, Bad Bugs"*

Think of what you know

You already know many things that help you when you read. You know that some insects attack trees and plants that give us food. But do any bugs help farmers? How? Talk about your ideas. Then write what you think this story will be about.

This selection describes the use of beneficial insects to combat insects that destroy crops and plants. Highlighted is the use of the *Hyposoter* wasp to kill army worms that threaten a broccoli crop. The selection explains that people have known about and used beneficial insects for over 2,000 years, but that most farmers today use pesticides as a quicker, easier way to control insects. Included also are the advantages and disadvantages of both pesticides and beneficial insects. Remind students of the crickets that attacked the Mormons' wheat crop in "Bird Heroes." Ask students what farmers and gardeners can do to keep insects from attacking their crops or plants.

Decide what you want to learn

Always read with questions in mind. Then you can look for answers to them. Look at the pictures on page 91. What do you think they show?

Students will probably note that a bug appears to be stinging a caterpillar. This is, in fact, a spined soldier bug using its stinger to paralyze a caterpillar before eating it.

Write one thing you hope to learn from this story.

Students may want to learn what good bugs do to bad bugs.

Get ready to use your reading skills

As you read, you need to put facts together. Sometimes a story does not tell you how all the facts fit. The questions in the green boxes will help you. They ask you to think about:

How things are alike or different. Can you compare things, events, people, or ideas to understand more about them?

Ideas not stated. The story hints at some new ideas. Can you use your own thinking to help you figure them out?

What the most important idea is. Can you find a sentence that tells the most important idea of the story?

Understand the words

Here are some words from "Good Bugs, Bad Bugs." Use the story and pictures to help you understand them.

beneficial **caterpillar** **ladybug** **pesticides**
broccoli **insects** **moths** **wasp**

To help students with new vocabulary, draw a chart on the chalkboard. Label one column **GOOD FOR FARMS** and the other **BAD FOR FARMS.** Discuss each new word as it relates to farms and crops and have students predict which column each term belongs in.

4 Reading

Good Bugs, Bad Bugs

John Martin has a farm in Jasper, Arkansas. One day he looked out at his fields. His young broccoli plants were completely covered with *army worms,* a kind of **caterpillar.** If they weren't stopped, they would eat all John's broccoli.

For the question below, John Martin let the wasps loose in his fields because he knew they would lay eggs inside the caterpillars and eventually kill them, thereby saving his broccoli crop.

Think About It

▷ Why do you think John let the wasps loose in his fields?

But John wasn't worried. He knew something that the caterpillars didn't know. At this very minute, an enemy was growing inside the caterpillars. It was slowly eating away at them. Soon, the caterpillars would die.

What was happening? There is a tiny wasp that is a born enemy of army worms. These wasps lay their eggs *inside* the caterpillars. Soon the eggs hatch. The new wasps eat the caterpillars from the inside out. John had let loose hundreds of these wasps in his fields.

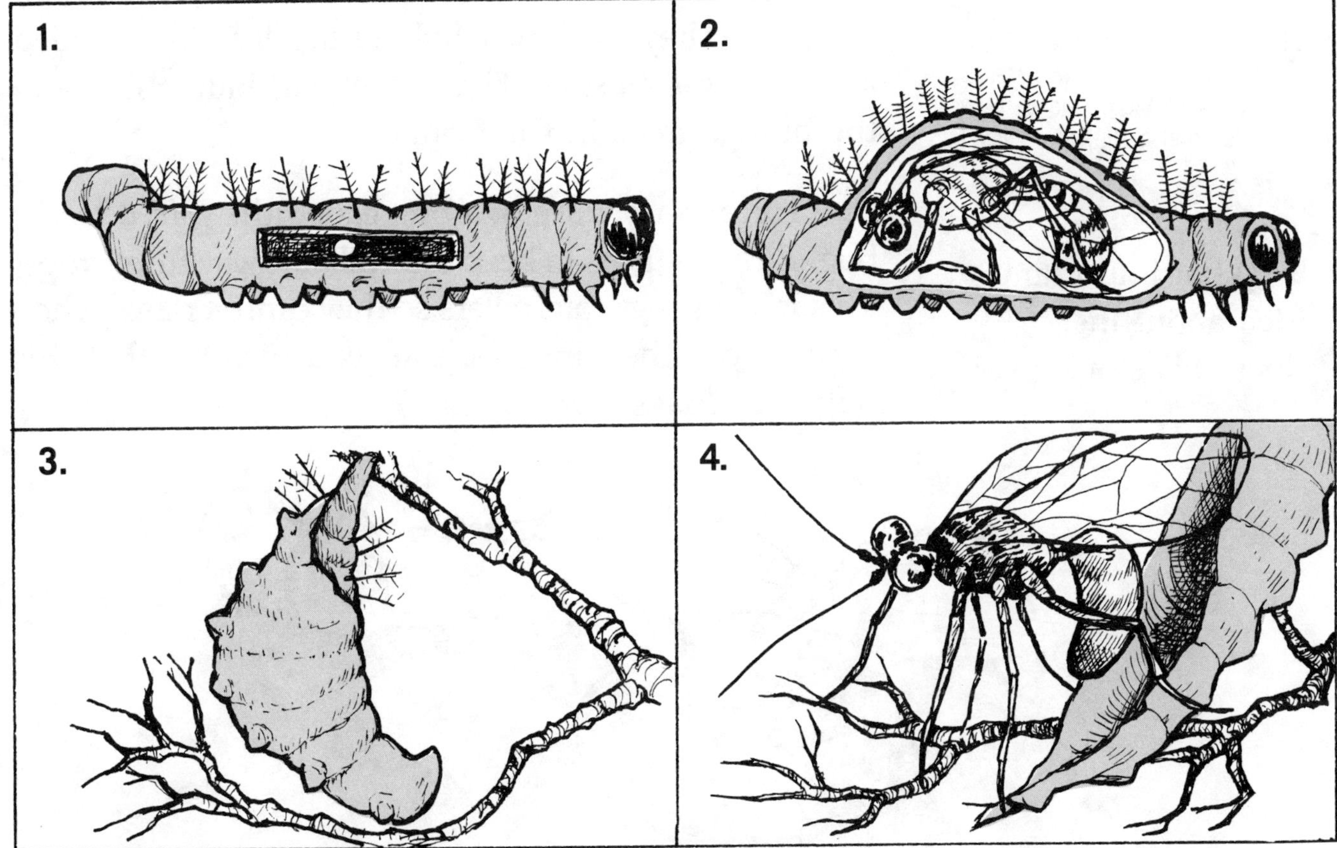

John watched this bug fight for over a month. After two weeks, the caterpillars stopped eating. They started to move more slowly. They looked sick. After four weeks, they started to spin soft shells. Caterpillars spin shells when they are about to turn into moths. But this time wasps, not moths, came bursting out of the shells! The caterpillars had all died. John's plants were saved. The good bugs had beaten the bad bugs.

Many people think all bugs are bad for gardens and farms. But farmers like John know that some bugs help farmers. Bad bugs eat vegetables, fruits, and other plants. Good bugs help farmers by eating the bad bugs. Scientists call good bugs **beneficial insects.** They *benefit*, or help, farmers.

People have known about beneficial insects for a long time. More than 2,000 years ago, farmers in China learned to put nests of ants in orange and lemon trees. The ants ate insects that came to eat the trees. In 1888, scientists brought a kind of ladybug to California from Australia. They used the ladybugs to kill an insect called a *cottony-cushion scale.* This insect was killing many of the orange trees in California.

Answers for the question below will vary. Beneficial insects help farmers by eating insects that destroy crops. You may want to model how students can review the details in the selection to help them figure out what the most important idea is. Point out also the difference between a main idea and a supporting detail.

Think About It

▷ What important idea about insects does this story give?

Here is a picture of a bug called the *spined soldier* bug. Farmers use it to keep caterpillars away from crops. This insect stings caterpillars so they cannot move. Then it sucks out their insides. Can you picture what this bug fight looks like up close?

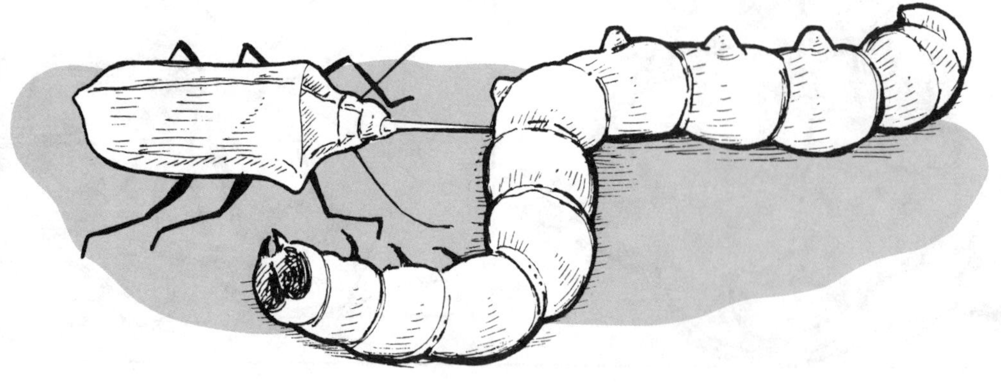

For the questions in the first box below: Beneficial insects are like pesticides in that they attack and kill crop-eating insects. Differences are: Beneficial insects are a natural way of controlling pests, whereas pesticides are not; pesticides work more quickly; pesticides can be harmful to people and the environment; and insects can get used to pesticides (continued below)

During the last 50 years, most farmers in this country have used **pesticides.** Pesticides are poisons that kill bad bugs. Pesticides are easy to use and work very well at first. But over time, insects often become used to them. Then it takes more and stronger pesticides to kill the bugs. This can cost a lot of money.

Think About It

▷ How are beneficial insects like pesticides? How are they different?

Think About It

▷ What do you think happens at a "bug farm"? How might a "bug farm" be like a regular farm? How might it be different?

Pesticides also can't tell the difference between insects that hurt crops and insects that plants need. Many plants use good bugs to spread their seeds. Without the bugs, these plants might not grow again the next year. And animals that eat plants coated with pesticides can get very sick, or even die. Another problem with pesticides is that they can hurt workers who touch them. People worry, too, about pesticides in our food and drinking water.

That's why many farmers are becoming interested in beneficial insects. Some farmers buy thousands of beneficial insects to put in their fields. They get these good bugs in the mail from "bug farms" that grow and sell them. As many as 80,000 ladybugs may be shipped to a farmer at one time!

over time. You may want to model how to compare two things by identifying the similarities and differences between them.

Answers will vary. Students may compare bug farms to farms that raise animals, including how insects and animals are cared for before being sold. Students may note that bug farms are probably much smaller than regular farms.

Think About It

▷ Look at the chart. Which good bugs would you want in your garden or field? Why?

Not all farmers buy beneficial insects from bug farms. Some farmers use the many good bugs that already live around farms. How do they do this? First, they stop using pesticides that kill good bugs. Then they plant some crops around their fields that good bugs like. These crops are not for eating. They're just to bring the good bugs. When the good bugs come, they find fields full of tasty bad bugs to eat!

Bad Bugs	Some Plants They Eat	Good Bugs to Fight Them
Aphids	Almost all plants	Ladybugs Praying mantids Lacewings
Japanese beetles	Corn, beans, berries, apples, plums, cherries, grapes	Assassin bugs 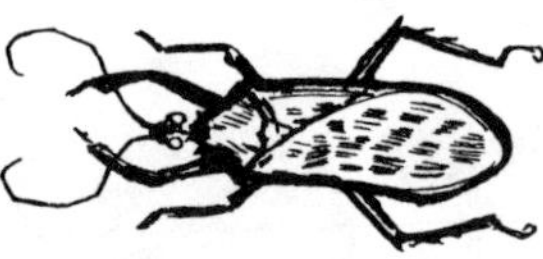
Mealybugs	Potatoes, cotton, pumpkins, oranges lemons, apples, pears	Ladybugs Lacewings 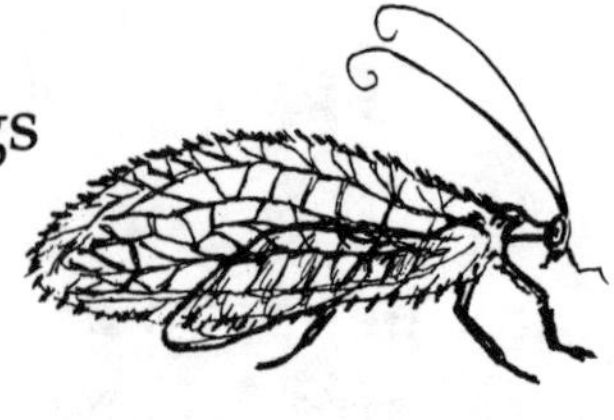
Mexican bean beetles 	All kinds of beans	Spined soldier bug

Answers will vary. Make sure students justify their choice of bugs.

The idea of using beneficial insects sounds very good. But there are some problems, too. Beneficial insects do not work as fast or as long as pesticides. Farmers have to plan carefully. They must be sure to have enough good bugs around for when they need them. This can be a lot of work. And sometimes good bugs are not enough. There could be a sudden, heavy attack of bad bugs. Then farmers might have to turn to pesticides to kill them all.

Answers for the question below will vary. Students should support their responses with information from the selection as well as their own experience and knowledge.

Think About It

▷ Which do you think are better, pesticides or beneficial insects?

Finally, remember one thing when you think about insects. In nature, no bug is really "good" or "bad." People call them good or bad because of what they do to crops. Really, all bugs just eat what they need to live.

Most farmers agree that something must be done to keep bugs away from crops. But which way is best? Both scientists and farmers are looking for this answer.

4 After reading *"Good Bugs, Bad Bugs"*

Think about the story

1. The pictures on page 91 show how tiny wasps attack army worms. Use those pictures to help you fill in the boxes of the flow chart below. Write the four steps to show what happens between the wasps and the army worms.

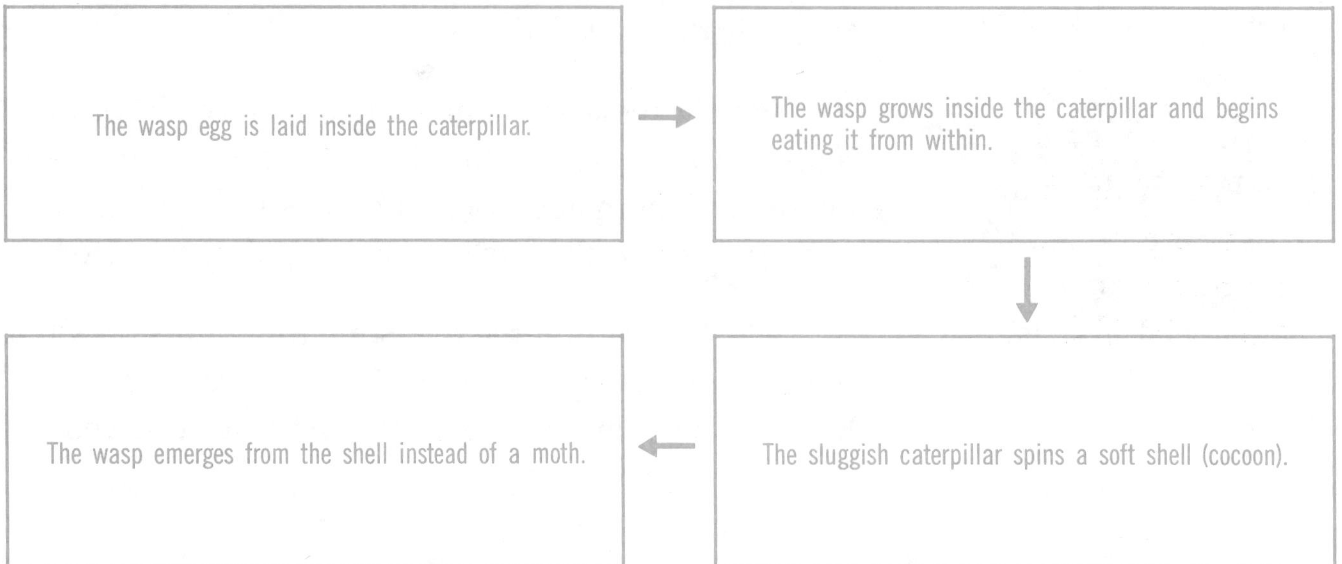

The wasp egg is laid inside the caterpillar.
The wasp grows inside the caterpillar and begins eating it from within.
The sluggish caterpillar spins a soft shell (cocoon).
The wasp emerges from the shell instead of a moth.

2. Suppose you want to tell someone about beneficial insects. What are the most important ideas you should explain?

Answers will vary, but might include some of the following points: Beneficial insects attack insects that are harmful to fruits, vegetables, and other plants; beneficial insects have been used for more than 2,000 years; there are many types of beneficial insects; bug farms are places where farmers and gardeners can buy beneficial insects.

3. Most farmers still use pesticides more than beneficial insects. Why do you think this is so?

Answers will vary. Possible responses include: Pesticides are easier to use; pesticides work more quickly; etc.

4. Look at the chart on page 94. Which good bugs could you use to kill aphids? Which would be good to kill Mexican bean beetles?

For aphids, use: ladybugs, praying mantids, lacewings

For Mexican bean beetles, use: spined soldier bug

Check what you learned

Turn back to page 90. Read again what you wanted to learn from this story. Did you find out what you wanted to know? If so, tell what you learned.

Answers will vary depending on the goals students set for themselves.

Were all your questions answered? If not, tell how you could find the answers.

Students may mention going to the library as a way to find answers to their questions. In addition, suggest that students look in the library for the books listed at the bottom of this page. Students might also write to bug farms, seed catalog companies, or *The Farmer's Almanac* for further information.

Use your own words

Pretend you are the size of a bug. You are crawling along the ground one day near a farm. Suddenly you see that a bug fight is going on! Write about it. The chart on page 94 will help you. Use a separate piece of paper and try to answer these questions:

- What crop is growing nearby?
- What kind of insect is eating the crop?
- What kind of insect is fighting the crop eater?
- Who wins?

You may want students to follow the steps of the writing process described on page T10 of this Annotated Teacher's Edition to complete this assignment. When they have finished their writing, invite students to share their completed stories with the class.

Find out more

Did you enjoy "Good Bugs, Bad Bugs"? If so, read more about beneficial insects. Look for these books in your library:

- Jobb, Jamie. *My Garden Companion.* Sierra Club Books/Charles Scribner's Sons, 1977.
- Parker, Nancy Winslow. *Bugs.* Greenwillow, 1987.

After reading *FARMING AND RANCHING COMMUNITIES*

Think about what you've learned

Read each question. Fill in the circle next to the best answer.

1. Many of these attack and destroy crops.
   - (A) insects
   - (B) prairie dogs
   - (C) cattle
   - (D) gulls

2. What do *beneficial insects* do?
   - (A) eat farmers' crops
   - (B) eat insects that eat crops
   - (C) spin soft shells
   - (D) attack sea gulls

3. Ants, prairie dogs, plants, and farmers all need this.
   - (A) city
   - (B) plow
   - (C) wheat
   - (D) soil

4. After the Civil War, cow towns grew
   - (A) along the Mormon Trail.
   - (B) along dry riverbeds.
   - (C) along new railroad lines.
   - (D) along old cattle trails.

Read each question. Write your answer on the lines.

5. Farmers and ranchers work very hard. Explain why their work is important.

Answers will vary. Students will probably note that farmers and ranchers provide food for the rest of the population. Without food, people would starve. And without the efforts of farmers and ranchers, all the people in the country would have to find their own food and wouldn't have time to do other important things.

6. What if you could live on a farm, on a ranch, in a cow town, or on a bug farm? Which place would you choose to live? Why?

Answers will vary. Make sure students explain their choice.

Write about what you've learned

Animals, insects, people, and plants all share the same land. Draw a picture that shows this happening. Under the picture, write some sentences about it. Use another piece of paper for your drawing and writing.

When students are finished, help them create a class book of their pictures and writing. You might title the book "How We Share Our Land."

DESERT COMMUNITIES

To start:
In the southwestern desert, dried stream beds, or *arroyos,* provide a drainage system. When the rains come, the arroyos fill with water which rushes down to the desert floor, sweeping rock, gravel, and sand before it. The water deposits this rock, sand, and gravel in fanlike shapes, called alluvial fans. Water also runs into dry lake beds, or *playas,* where it will either seep into the ground or evaporate under the desert sun. Discuss with students what happens to the water when it rains where you live. Then encourage anyone who has lived in or visited a desert region to tell the class what it's like.

A rabbit sits perfectly still on the hard, dry land. Its ears move back and forth. Something is happening. Suddenly lightning leaps across the sky. Thunder rolls through nearby hills. The desert grows dark as clouds block the sun. The rabbit takes cover.

The first drop of rain hits the dusty ground. Then another and another, faster and faster. Soon the rain pours down. In minutes, wide streams of rushing water race across the desert floor. Flash flood! The flood carries everything with it. Then, just as quickly, the rain slows. The sky grows light again. The rainfall comes to an end. It will not rain again for many months.

The sudden storm brings both death and life. Plants are pulled up by the roots. Animals die in the raging water. But the water also helps other plants and animals to live. Soon after the storm, the desert blooms. Beautiful flowers cover the land.

You already know something about living in deserts

Think. Write some words that tell about a desert.

Answers will vary. Possibilities include: cactus, sagebrush, rattlesnake, gila monster, jackrabbit, dunes, canyons, etc.

Answers will vary. Students may say deserts are hot and dry; snakes coyotes, jackrabbits, and lizards live there; and they have heard about the Mojave, Sonoran, Sahara, Gobi, or Death Valley.

Talk. Share your ideas. Talk with a few classmates. See who can answer these questions.

- What is a desert like?
- What lives in a desert?
- What is the name of one desert you know of?

Write. Why might it be hard for people to live in a desert? What problems might they have? Write your ideas on another piece of paper.

Encourage students to share their writing with the class. You might list some of the problems mentioned on the chalkboard so students can assess the accuracy of their predictions after they have completed the unit.

New words, new uses

Some of the words in this unit may be new to you. Keep them in mind as you read the stories to come.

adobe: a brick made of clay and straw and hardened in the sun
oasis: a place in the desert with water, trees, and plants
rainfall: the amount of rain that falls in a place
region: a part of the earth's land area

Predicting

Here are the names of the stories in Unit Four. Read them and look at the picture below. Then write three things you think you might learn from the stories.

Anasazi: Ancient People of the Desert

Using Water

Santa Fe: Old Town, New Town

This, Too, Is Desert

Students will learn about: (1) the Anasazi settlements in the Four Corners; (2) how horned lizards and saguaro cacti obtain, store, and save water; (3) the history of Santa Fe, New Mexico; and (4) what constitutes a desert, and where deserts are found throughout the world.

New information

After you have finished this unit, you will know the answers to these questions and more:

- Who built homes in the sides of huge cliffs?
- How do plants and animals live in the desert?
- What is the history of Santa Fe?
- Are all deserts the same?

Encourage students to examine the illustration and tell what it shows about life in the desert. Ask them if they've ever seen plants like those in the picture, for example, and what they think those buildings in the background are.

1 Before reading *"Anasazi: Ancient People of the Desert"*

Think of what you know

You already know many things that help you when you read. Look at the title of this story. How could people long ago have lived in a desert with very little water and few plants? Talk about your ideas. Then write what you think this story will be about.

This selection opens with a description of the Four Corners region of the American Southwest, focusing on the ruins of Mesa Verde. It explains that Mesa Verde was built by the Anasazi, whose oldest known settlement was in Chaco Canyon, New Mexico. The selection then describes Chaco Canyon and the Anasazi's irrigation systems. It discusses Anasazi movement throughout the Four Corners, and offers reasons for that movement: perhaps a great drought and the definite exhaustion of the land due to intensive use. Discuss with students what they think life in the desert is like today. Then ask what it might have been like hundreds of years ago. How were people able to survive?

Decide what you want to learn

Always read with questions in mind. Then you can look for answers to them. Look at the picture on page 103. What do you think it shows?

The photograph is of Pueblo Bonito in the Chaco Canyon settlement. It shows the interconnectedness of the various units and the Anasazi building style.

Write one thing you hope to learn from this story.

Students might be curious to learn who the Anasazi were and how they managed to live in the desert.

Get ready to use your reading skills

As you read, you need to put facts together. Sometimes a story does not tell you how all the facts fit. The questions in the green boxes will help you. They ask you to think about:

Why things happen. Can you figure out why something happens in a story? Can you see what happens because of it?

How things are alike or different. Can you compare things, events, people, or ideas to understand more about them?

Your own thoughts. Can your own thoughts help you judge what the story says?

Understand the words

Here are some words from "Anasazi: Ancient People of the Desert." Use the story and pictures to help you understand them.

adobe	**cliff**	**drought**
canyon	**ditches**	**region**

To help students with new vocabulary, discuss with them each new word in terms of its relation to desert geography and life. You might also draw on the chalkboard pictures of a cliff dwelling and an adobe house to help students visualize them. *National Geographic* (Feb., 1964) has a pictorial article on the Anasazi.

1 **Reading**

Anasazi: Ancient People of the Desert

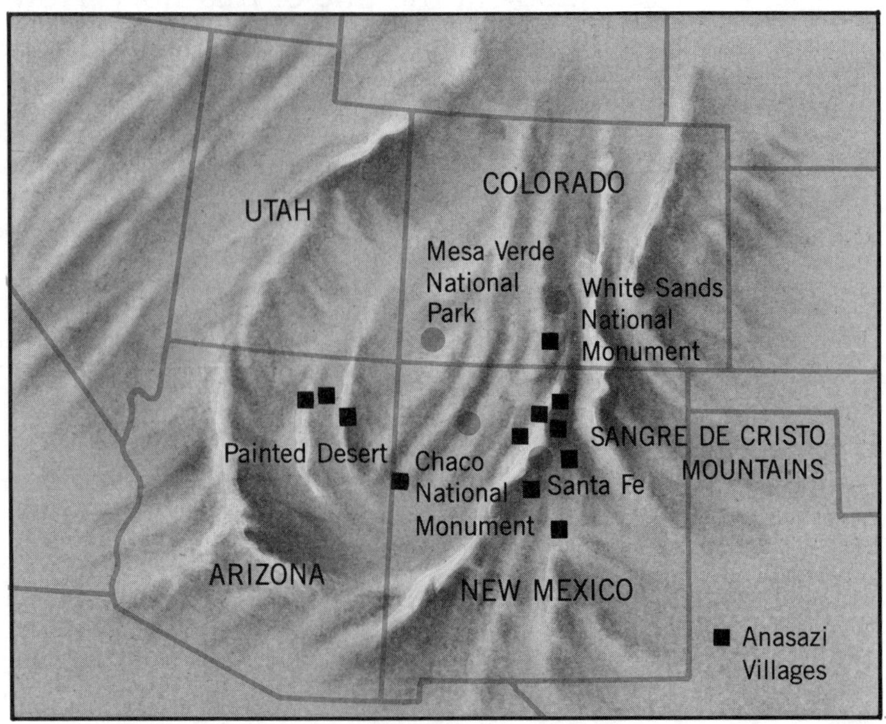

For the question below, students may conclude that a harsh climate and very little water would make living in the desert extremely difficult. Ask students what it would be like to try to live off the land in a desert.

> **Think About It**
> ▷ Why do most deserts have very few towns and cities?

Look at the map. Find the place where four states touch each other. This is called the Four Corners region. It is a desert—high, flat, and very dry. Today it is a lonely place. If you see something move, it is probably a rabbit or a snake.

But if you take a back road to the Mancos River you will come to a place called Mesa Verde. There you'll see an amazing sight. The river runs through a deep canyon. On the sides of the canyon are caves. And in the caves are hundreds of stone houses. Some are four stories high, with many rooms. Some even have towers. Many of the towers have fallen down now, though. And the stone walls have big holes in them. No one has lived here for more than 700 years.

> **Think About It**
> ▷ Why might people decide to build houses in caves on the side of a canyon?

Who built this fine city in such a strange place? The answer is the **Anasazi** (ahn-uh-SAHZ-ee). That is a Navajo word for these Native Americans. It means "strangers who lived long ago."

Possible answers include: Houses were built in caves or on cliffs so the people who lived there could be protected from enemies; caves were probably much cooler than the desert floor. Lead students to realize that their own thinking can help them understand what they read.

Anasazi houses have been found in many parts of the Four Corners. But the oldest and largest villages were in Chaco Canyon. This is a long, narrow valley in New Mexico, near Arizona.

Scientists think the Anasazi began building homes in Chaco Canyon about 900 A.D. They founded 12 large villages there and many smaller ones as well. These villages are not in a cliff wall. They are in the open. All the houses in each village are joined together to make one giant house.

For the question below, students might note that adobe was a good material because it could be made nearby with things the Anasazi found around them. It also served as a "glue" to hold rocks together. The Anasazi had to go to the mountains for logs because very few trees grew in the desert.

Think About It

▷ Why was adobe mud a good building material for the Anasazi to use? Why did the Anasazi go all the way to the mountains to get logs?

The walls of the Chaco buildings are made of small, flat pieces of stone. The Anasazi carefully fitted the stones together. Adobe mud helped to hold them in place. Sticks and more mud made the roofs, which were held up by huge logs. The Anasazi had to bring some of these logs from mountains about 50 miles away. Many roads led from the mountains to the valley. Roads also ran between the valley villages.

The largest building in Chaco Canyon is called *Pueblo Bonito.* This means "beautiful village" in Spanish. Pueblo Bonito is really a giant apartment house. It is five stories high in places. It has about 800 rooms. A whole family probably lived in each room. Over 1,000 people may have lived in Pueblo Bonito at one time. Chaco Canyon itself probably held about 10,000 people.

Think About It

▷ Why do you think people today care about places where ancient peoples lived?

Before students answer, you might have them discuss whether studying the past can provide any lessons about the present or future. Students may recognize that learning about ancient places can help us understand ourselves and others. It is also very enjoyable for many people.

The Anasazi were farmers. Like other Native Americans of the Southwest, they grew corn, beans, and squash. To get such a dry land to feed so many people, the Anasazi dug long ditches. The ditches carried water down from the mountains each spring, when the snow melted.

Scientists think the Anasazi began to leave Chaco Canyon around 1100 A.D. Some of them may have gone to Colorado to join other Anasazi. Scientists do know that not long after that, the Anasazi in Colorado began to build the cliff houses at Mesa Verde above the Mancos River.

The Anasazi's good life at Mesa Verde ended suddenly around 1300 A.D. In about 20 years' time, the great apartment houses emptied. The people seemed just to disappear. Scientists think many may have moved farther south. Some probably went to the Rio Grande Valley in Texas. Others may have been the fathers and mothers of the Hopi and Zuni peoples of Arizona and New Mexico.

Think About It

▷ What clues might have helped scientists figure out where the Anasazi went after they left Mesa Verde?

Clues might include: similar settlements in new locations, similar pots and tools in new places, signs of trails or other evidence leading to the new settlements. Help students understand that scientists piece together many clues to arrive at conclusions, but that these conclusions may change as new information is discovered.

Why did the Anasazi leave? The main reason may have been a great **drought.** It lasted from about 1275 to 1300. Think of trying to do without rain for 25 years! Still, the Anasazi had lived through other long droughts. This one may have driven them away because they were fighting other Native American peoples at the same time.

The Anasazi had learned how to live in the desert very well. They had learned how to get enough food from the dry land to feed many people. They had learned how to use the land's sticks and stones and mud to make huge "apartment houses." They had learned how to use its rocky cliffs to keep their homes and families safe. Yet the Anasazi may have used the land too well. They cut down its trees for firewood. They used water from wells until the wells went dry. They took all that the land had to give. When it could give no more, the Anasazi were forced to leave.

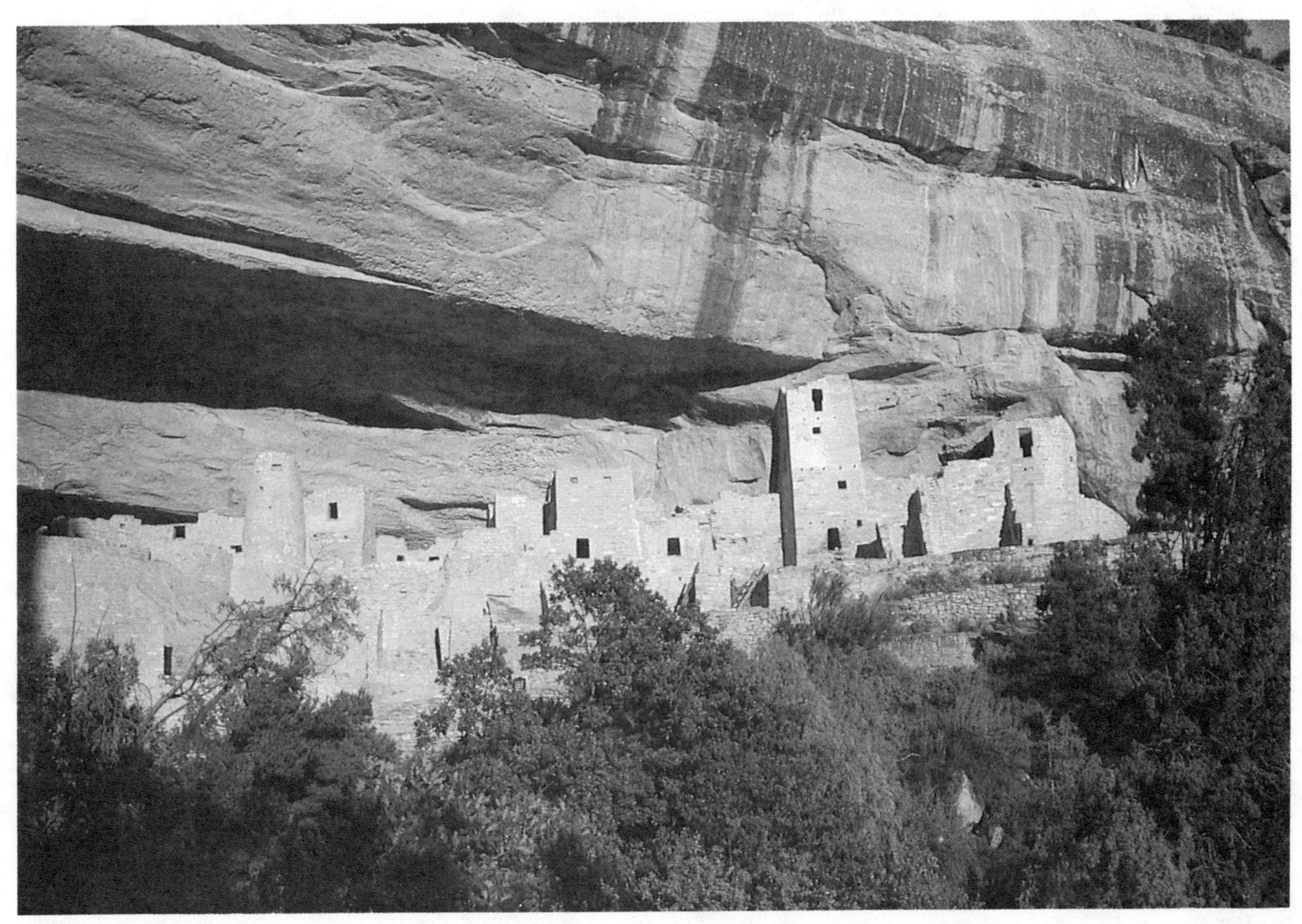

1 After reading *"Anasazi: Ancient People of the Desert"*

Think about the story

1. What is the land like in the Four Corners region? What is the weather like? Think about what you just read. Then fill in the web below.

Answers will vary. Possibilities include:

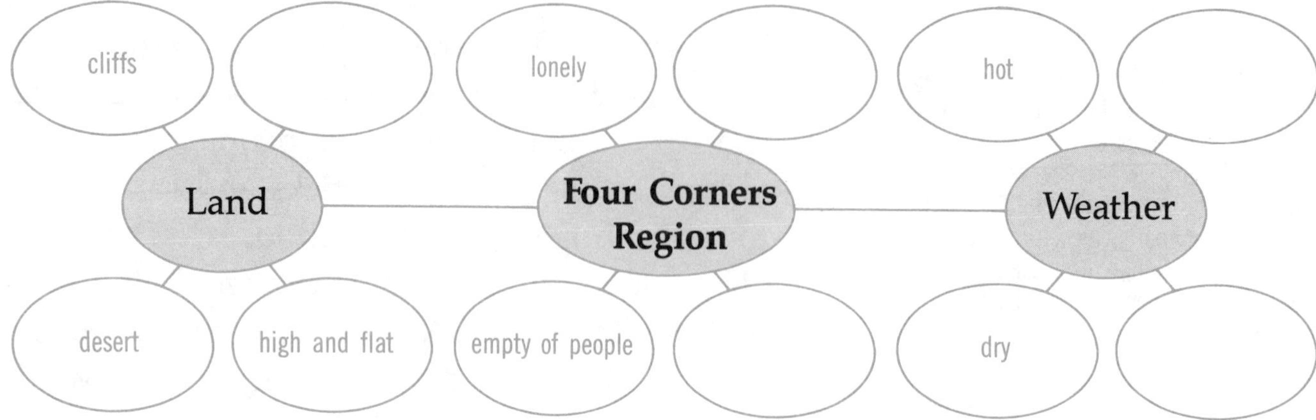

2. How were the Anasazi's houses different from our houses? What made them good homes?

They were made mainly of rock and adobe, and they were sometimes joined together to make one large house. Some had many stories and rooms, with a whole family in each room. They were good homes because they were well built and lasted a long time. Help students realize that the homes also must have been good because the communities they were in grew and prospered for many years. By comparing and contrasting their own homes with Anasazi dwellings, students should recognize that different types of buildings and materials are suited to different places, times, and people.

3. Scientists think the Anasazi began to leave Chaco Canyon around 1100 A.D. List some possible reasons for their move.

Answers will vary. Possibilities include: The Anasazi may have moved because of a great drought, or because other Native American people came and attacked them. Factors such as natural disasters, disease, or crop failure may also have prompted a move. Encourage students to use their own thoughts to draw conclusions about information in the selection.

4. What if the Anasazi had moved to a place where there were many trees and plenty of water? How do you think their way of life might have been different?

Answers will vary. Perhaps the Anasazi would have built different kinds of buildings, using wood rather than rock and adobe. They also might have grown different kinds of food in different ways, or have spent more time hunting and fishing. Perhaps life would have been easier for everyone in the area, and there would have been less reason to fear attack from their neighbors.

Check what you learned

Turn back to page 101. Read again what you wanted to learn from this story. Did you find out what you wanted to know? If so, tell what you learned.

Answers will vary depending on the goals students set for themselves.

Were all your questions answered? If not, tell how you could find the answers.

Students may mention going to the library as a way to find answers to their questions. They might also visit a museum, particularly one with exhibits of early or prehistoric cultures. In addition, direct students' attention to the books listed at the bottom of this page.

Use your own words

You just read about a city built on the side of a cliff. This city, Mesa Verde, is different from almost every other city ever built. Imagine what it would have been like to live there. Then write a story about it on another piece of paper. You might write about one of the following ideas:

- Teaching a brother or sister how to get from place to place
- Helping build a new house
- Helping to plant crops
- Keeping safe from an attack by another group of Native Americans

You may want students to follow the steps of the writing process described on page T10 of this Annotated Teacher's Edition to complete their writing. When students have finished, suggest that they illustrate their stories. Then invite students to share their work with the class.

Find out more

Did you enjoy "Anasazi: Ancient People of the Desert"? If so, read more about the Anasazi. Look for these books in your library:

- Bowyer, Carol. *The Children's Book of Houses and Homes.* Usborne, 1978.
- Weiss, Harvey. *Shelters: From Teepee to Igloo.* Thomas Y. Crowell, 1988.
- Wolfson, Evelyn. *From Abenaki to Zuni: A Dictionary of Native American Tribes.* Walker, 1988.
- Yue, Charlotte. *The Pueblo.* Knopf, 1984.

2 Before reading *"Using Water"*

Think of what you know

You already know many things that help you when you read. You know that all living things need water. How could desert plants and animals get or save water? Talk about your ideas. Then write what you think this story will be about.

This selection describes the ways in which two living things—the horned toad and the saguaro cactus—find and save water in the desert. Explain to students that desert animals and plants have special ways to find and save water. Invite them to speculate on what these ways might be.

Decide what you want to learn

Always read with questions in mind. Then you can look for answers to them. Look at the picture on page 110. What is happening?

The illustration shows a horned lizard defending itself against a coyote by shooting blood from its eyes.

Write one thing you hope to learn from this story.

Students may want to know how animals and plants of the desert are able to survive.

Get ready to use your reading skills

As you read, you need to put facts together. Sometimes a story does not tell you how all the facts fit. The questions in the green boxes will help you. They ask you to think about:

How things are alike or different. Can you compare things, events, people, or ideas to understand more about them?

Ideas not stated. The story hints at some new ideas. Can you use your own thinking to help you figure them out?

What the most important idea is. Can you find a sentence that tells the most important idea of the story?

Understand the words

Here are some words from "Using Water." Use the story and pictures to help you understand them.

adapted	**deserts**	**gallon**	**sweat**
breathe	**dew**	**lizard**	**thorns**
cactus	**eyelids**		

To help students with new vocabulary, write the new words on the chalkboard. Divide the class into groups, giving each group one of the words. Tell the groups to discuss the word among themselves (using a dictionary if necessary) and prepare three clues about its meaning. Then have the groups present their clues to the class until the word is correctly identified.

2 Reading

Using Water

In the deserts of the American Southwest, one animal shoots streams of blood from its eyes. This is not a monster from a movie. It is *real!*

Scientists have gone to see this animal. Its skin is hard and dry. Pointed horns cover its whole body. It looks like one of the scariest things on earth.

This is the **horned lizard.** It is very small. It eats ants and other small bugs. It could never hurt a person.

The horned lizard is *not* a monster. But it is perfectly suited to life in the desert. In a desert, you would soon die if you couldn't find water to drink. But a horned lizard can go a long time without drinking.

Think About It

▷ How do you think the horned lizard can go a long time without drinking?

Possible answers include: It is very small, so it doesn't need much water; it sweats less because it has fewer and smaller holes in its skin; it loses less water through breathing because it spends time underground, out of the sun. Make sure students can justify their responses.

How does it do this? First of all, the horned lizard saves more water than people do. When you sweat, water passes through tiny holes in your skin into the air. When you breathe, water goes out of your mouth and nose into the air. The hotter it is outside, the more water you lose in these ways.

The horned lizard has fewer and smaller holes in its skin than people do. So it loses very little water through sweat. It also likes to dig under the ground to shade its body from the sun. In this way, it does not lose as much water through breathing.

For the question in the first box below: It probably drinks more water from dew than from rain, since dew is more common in the desert than rain. Remind students that they can use their own thinking to figure out ideas that are not exactly given in the selection.

Think About It

▷ Which does the horned lizard probably drink more often, water from dew or water from rain?

The horned lizard also has interesting ways of getting water. One way is through its food. All living things have water in their bodies. So the horned lizard gets water out of the ants and other bugs it eats.

Another way it gets water is from **dew.** Dew is small drops of water that come out of the air at night. In the morning, the horned lizard licks this dew off plants. And when it does rain, the horned lizard drinks drops of water that fall on the tops of rocks. One kind of horned lizard, the Texas horned lizard, can even collect drops of rain between the horny bumps on its back. Then the water slides down its back into the corners of its mouth!

Think About It

▷ Why do horned lizards shoot blood from their eyes? When might they do this?

You may still be wondering how and why the horned lizard shoots blood from its eyes. Only a few kinds of horned lizards can do this. First they close their eyes. Then they fill their eyelids with blood. Finally, they push out their eyes. This makes a fine stream of blood shoot out. It may fly as far as four feet. Coyotes and foxes hate the taste of this blood. They won't eat the lizard even if they're really hungry.

They shoot blood when they are in danger from other animals such as coyotes and foxes. These other animals don't like the taste of the lizard's blood, so they try to avoid it.

Plants have also adapted to life in the deserts of the Southwest. The **saguaro cactus** may not look as frightening as the horned lizard. But the saguaro is certainly big and strange enough to be a monster. In fact, it is the largest kind of cactus in the United States. It may grow up to 50 feet tall. Its base can grow to nearly 3 feet wide. It can weigh 20,000 pounds!

For the question below, the most important idea is that the saguaro works like a giant water balloon.

Think About It

▷ What is the most important idea of this paragraph?

The saguaro works like a giant water balloon. It has many thin, long roots that lie just under the ground. When it rains, these roots pull water out of the ground. They bring the water to the saguaro. Then the plant puffs up. Its trunk and branches stretch open to let it hold even more water. The saguaro stores this water and uses it just a little at a time. The next rain might not come for a whole year!

How does the saguaro save its water from the hot air? It has fat skin and no leaves. The thin skin on the leaves of trees has lots of tiny holes to let in air. (Plants need air to make food.) But these holes also let out lots of water. A tree with 200,000 leaves can lose 700 to 900 gallons of water in one day through its leaves.

A saguaro has only a few small air holes. It opens these in the morning and evening, when it is cool. At these times it collects air and stores it inside, like water. In this way, a saguaro loses less than half a gallon of water a day through its skin.

The saguaro is also covered with long thorns. These make some shade for the plant. They also stop animals from chewing on the plant to get at its water.

Think About It

▷ How are saguaros like trees? How are they different?

So you see, the horned lizard and the saguaro make a fine pair. They are both good at getting and saving water in deserts, where water is very hard to come by.

Saguaros are like trees because both are large plants, both have thick trunks and branches, and both have holes in them that allow them to take in air. But the saguaro has fewer holes, and it only opens them in the morning and evening, when it is cool. In this way it loses less water. Encourage the students to draw on their own knowledge to help them with their comparisons.

2 After reading *"Using Water"*

Think about the story

1. The horned lizard has many things that let it live in places with little water. Write *true* beside each thing below that helps it get or save water.

   ___true___ It has few holes in its skin.

   ________ It shoots blood from its eyes.

   ___true___ It licks drops of water off plants.

   ___true___ It eats ants and other small bugs.

2. How might the horned lizard's hard, horny skin help it survive? Try to think of two different ways.

Answers will vary. Possibilities include: It would help the lizard protect itself against attackers and against the rocks and harsh sun of the desert; the skin might help the lizard blend in with the rocks and dirt of the desert, so its enemies wouldn't notice it; the hard skin might help the lizard retain water in its body.

3. The saguaro's roots do not go deep into the ground. Instead, they lie near the top of the ground. Why do you think this is so?

Before students begin, you might have them think about where the little amount of water that is found in the desert generally comes from—dew and rain. The saguaro's roots stay close to the top of the ground so that they can soak up even the smallest amount of rain or dew before it dries.

4. How are horned lizards and saguaros alike?

Both are good at getting and saving water, and at surviving in the desert. One specific similarity is that both have few holes in their skin. This helps them save water.

   How are they different?

The main difference between a horned lizard and a saguaro is that the lizard is an animal and the saguaro is a plant. Saguaros get water through their roots, while horned lizards get it from their food or from catching dew.

Check what you learned

Turn back to page 108. Read again what you wanted to learn from this story. Did you find out what you wanted to know? If so, tell what you learned.

Answers will vary depending on the goals students set for themselves.

Were all your questions answered? If not, tell how you could find the answers.

Students may mention going to the library as a way to find answers to their questions. Also, if possible, they might visit a science or natural history museum. In addition, suggest that students find and read the books listed at the bottom of this page.

Use your own words

Pretend you are a coyote wandering through the desert. You are hungry and thirsty. Suddenly you see a horned lizard and a saguaro cactus. Tell what happens when you try to eat them. Use a separate piece of paper and try to answer these questions:

- How do you feel?
- Can you think of a way to eat the lizard?
- Why might you want to eat the cactus?
- Can you think of a way to eat the cactus?

You may want students to follow the steps of the writing process described on page T10 of this Annotated Teacher's Edition to complete this activity. Invite students to share their completed stories with the class.

Find out more

Did you enjoy "Using Water"? If so, read more about lizards and cactuses. Look for these books in your library:

- Heller, Ruth. *How to Hide a Crocodile and Other Reptiles.* Grosset and Dunlap, 1986.
- McConnell, Keith. *ReptAlphabet.* Stemmer, 1982.
- Overbeck, Cynthia. *Cactus.* Lerner, 1982.

3 Before reading *"Santa Fe: Old Town, New Town"*

Think of what you know

You already know many things that help you when you read. Do you know where Santa Fe is? Do you know how old a city it is? Who might have been the first people to live there? Talk about your ideas. Then write what you think this story will be about.

This selection traces the history of Santa Fe, New Mexico, from the earliest Native American settlements, through the Spanish and Mexican occupations, to its current status as a U.S. city. Have students tell what they know about the different people who settled the American continent, starting with Native Americans. Explain that people came to America from all over the world and many people from Spain and Mexico settled in the American Southwest. Point out Santa Fe on a map and ask students to tell why it might be a desirable location for a settlement. You might also remind students that in Unit Two they read about another city founded by the Spaniards, St. Augustine, Florida ("How Does a City Grow?"). As they read about Santa Fe, encourage students to compare it with St. Augustine.

Decide what you want to learn

Always read with questions in mind. Then you can look for answers to them. Look at the picture on page 117. What do you think is happening?

The illustration shows the residents of Santa Fe celebrating Mexico's independence from Spain.

Write one thing you hope to learn from this story.

Students may want to know if the Anasazi lived in Santa Fe. (There is evidence of Anasazi settlement around 1000 A.D.)

Get ready to use your reading skills

As you read, you need to put facts together. Sometimes a story does not tell you how all the facts fit. The questions in the green boxes will help you. They ask you to think about:

What happens next. Can you use your own thinking and story clues to tell what will happen next?

What people are feeling. Can you put yourself in another person's place? Can you imagine what that person feels or thinks?

Where the facts lead. You already know some facts. Others are given in the story. Can you put them together to figure out new ideas?

Understand the words

Here are some words from "Santa Fe: Old Town, New Town." Use the story and pictures to help you understand them.

adobe	**ditches**	**laws**	**settlers**
capital	**governor**	**plaza**	**soldiers**

To help students with new vocabulary, have them discuss each word as it might relate to the establishment and development of a community in the Southwest.

3 Reading

Santa Fe: Old Town, New Town

Many of our country's oldest cities are in the deserts of the Southwest. One of the oldest is in New Mexico. Santa Fe was a Native American village long before the Spaniards founded St. Augustine in Florida.

Think About It

▷ Why do you think many of our oldest cities are in the Southwest?

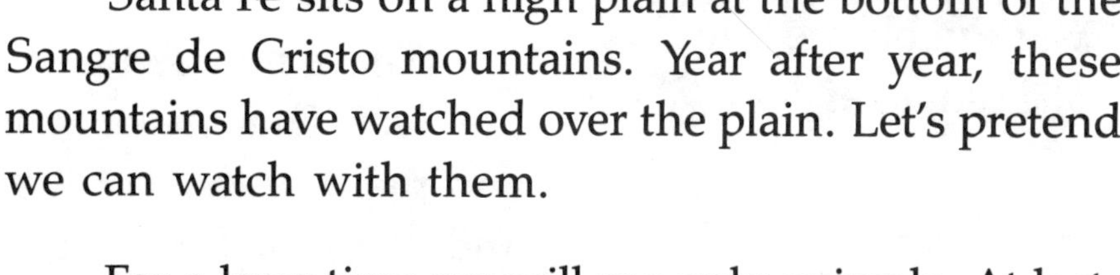

Santa Fe sits on a high plain at the bottom of the Sangre de Cristo mountains. Year after year, these mountains have watched over the plain. Let's pretend we can watch with them.

For a long time we will see only animals. At last, Native Americans come. They camp and hunt and move on. But some of them decide to stay. They plant corn and other vegetables. At the foot of the mountains, they build homes of dried mud.

Answers will vary. Possibilities include: The Spaniards came to the New World in the early 1500s and explored Mexico and the southern part of what would become the United States. They established cities along their route in order to control the area and to supply further explorations. Remind students of their earlier discussion of the settling of the American continent if they have difficulty drawing conclusions.

Hundreds of years pass. It is around 1000 A.D. The people build more villages on the plains and under mountain cliffs. Some of these villages are made of rock. They will last a long, long time. The people have become good farmers. They make beautiful things to wear and use. We can see their fires burning and hear their songs of thanks.

Later, more people come here from the north. All these Native Americans are known as the Pueblo people. Their plain is "the place where the sun dances."

Think About It

▷ Do you think the Pueblo people worried when they saw the Spaniards coming? Why or why not?

▷ How do you think the lives of the Pueblo people will change?

Answers to the first two questions will vary. Some students may say that the Pueblo people did worry, especially since the Spaniards claimed the land for themselves. Others may say that the Pueblo people might not have worried at first, since they didn't have any particular reason to fear the Spaniards. Make sure students can support their answers.

Answers to the last question will vary. Many students will probably predict that the Spaniards will treat the Pueblo people badly—like slaves. Ask students what they based their predictions on, and point out that what they already know can help them to predict what will happen.

It is now the 1540s. New people come to the plain, riding on strange animals never seen here before. They are Spanish soldiers who have come from Mexico City to look for riches. They are riding horses. They say that this land now belongs to the Spanish king.

Years pass. One day, lots of wagons come from the south. The wagons bring families and more soldiers. They stop at "the place where the sun dances." The year is 1610.

These new settlers dig ditches to carry water from the river. They make adobe bricks. They build a village and plant beans, corn, and red peppers. Their sheep and cows walk through the village streets. They call their village *la Villa de Santa Fe de San Francisco.*

The Spaniards leave an open place called a **plaza** in the middle of town. Next to the plaza, they build a palace for the governor to live in. Santa Fe is now the capital of New Mexico.

More and more Spanish settlers arrive. The town keeps growing. But the Pueblo people are not happy. They are told to change their ways. They are made to work in the fields. So one day they tell each other this must stop. Together they drive the Spaniards out of New Mexico.

For the next 12 years, Santa Fe is again a Pueblo village. But then a great many Spanish soldiers come marching from the south. The Pueblo people lose their village. Once again wagon trains bring Spanish families to Santa Fe.

These families build new houses, shops, and tall white churches. All have flat roofs and are one story high. The village becomes three streets wide and a mile long.

For the question below: They were glad because Spanish rule had been strict, Spain was far away, and most people probably wanted to rule themselves. Remind students that putting themselves in another person's place and imagining what that person is feeling or thinking can help them understand and appreciate the events in a story.

Think About It

▷ Why do you think the people of New Mexico were glad to throw off Spain's rule?

Wagons come often from Mexico City. They carry fine goods like glasses, books, and dresses. No wagons come from the United States, though. The Spaniards have passed laws against Americans coming into New Mexico.

Many more years pass. Watching from the mountains, we can hear shots being fired. People rush outside in their best clothes. For five days, they have parties and dance in the streets. Mexico has decided it no longer belongs to Spain. The year is 1821. People clap when Mexico's new flag goes up in the plaza.

For the first time, heavy wagons roll in from the east. New laws let Americans buy and sell in New Mexico. The wagons bring in all kinds of goods. They carry away furs and gold and silver. The road they travel is called the Santa Fe Trail.

Soon, Santa Fe begins to spread farther into the plain. Many people pass through it now. Some come to buy and sell, and some are on their way to California. American, German, and French voices ring in the streets.

One day in 1848, American soldiers take down the Mexican flag in the middle of town. They raise the flag of the United States. A war between Mexico and the United States has just ended. Now most of the Southwest belongs to the United States.

For the question below, answers will vary. Some students may say that the people in Santa Fe would look forward to the good things American rule would bring, such as more chances to trade and make money. Others may say that, as Spanish-speaking Mexicans, many people in Santa Fe would feel sad that their city was no longer a part of Mexico. They would worry about what life would be like under American rule, which was very foreign to them.

Think About It

▷ How do you think the people of Santa Fe felt when the American flag went up?

Taller wood buildings spring up next to the old adobe ones. New tracks are laid over the mountains. The railroad comes to Santa Fe and then goes on and on. Soon we can look down from the mountains at night and see streets full of lights.

Now let's look down on Santa Fe today. How big it is and different! The sun dances on the glass walls of tall new buildings. But if we look past them, we can see white and brown adobe walls. See? The old governor's palace is still there. Santa Fe is now a busy new city. But its long and colorful past is still there.

1000 A.D. Native Americans build stone villages on the plain around Santa Fe.

1540 The first Spanish soldiers come to New Mexico.

1610 Spaniards build a village and name it Santa Fe.

1680 The Pueblo people take over Santa Fe.

1692 Spanish soldiers take back Santa Fe.

1821 New Mexico becomes part of Mexico as the Mexicans gain independence from Spain.

1848 The United States takes over New Mexico.

1880 The train comes to Santa Fe.

1912 New Mexico becomes a state.

3 After reading *"Santa Fe: Old Town, New Town"*

Think about the story

1. Many different peoples have lived in Santa Fe. How did each group help Santa Fe become what it is today—a modern American city?

To help students respond, you might have them consider how different groups of people have changed, or might change, life in your own community. In Santa Fe, Native Americans, Spaniards, and Mexicans left their marks on many aspects of cultural and social life: building styles, place names, arts and crafts, food, clothing, music, holidays and celebrations, religion, etc.

2. Imagine that the Spaniards never came to New Mexico. How do you think the history of Santa Fe would have been different?

Answers will vary. Students may say that the Pueblo people would have continued to live in and near Santa Fe until the Americans arrived, and that today Santa Fe would not show the effects of Spanish rule in such things as buildings, names, and food.

3. The chart below shows some of the things that changed Santa Fe. Finish the chart. Tell how each event changed the city.

Soldiers came and said that the land belonged to the Spanish king.	The Spaniards founded the city of Santa Fe and ruled over the area.
The Pueblo people drove the Spaniards out of New Mexico.	The Pueblo people controlled Santa Fe for the next 12 years.
Mexico threw off the rule of Spain.	Mexico ruled Santa Fe and let Americans come in.
The United States took over Santa Fe after a war with Mexico.	Santa Fe has been part of the United States ever since.

Check what you learned

Turn back to page 114. Read again what you wanted to learn from this story. Did you find out what you wanted to know? If so, tell what you learned.

Answers will vary depending on the goals students set for themselves.

Were all your questions answered? If not, tell how you could find the answers.

Students may mention going to the library as a way to find answers to their questions. In addition, direct students' attention to the books listed at the bottom of this page.

Use your own words

Santa Fe changed a lot through the years. At what time would you have liked to live there? Pick one time and pretend you lived then. Write a story about it on a separate piece of paper. You might write about one of these ideas:

- Life in a Pueblo village: learning to make pots, or seeing the Spaniards ride in on their horses
- Life in the Spanish town: helping on a farm, or meeting a Pueblo boy or girl
- Life in the Mexican town: celebrating the end of Spanish rule, or watching wagons arrive
- Life in the American town: seeing American settlers move in, or watching the first train come to town

You may want students to follow the steps of the writing process described on page T10 of this Annotated Teacher's Edition. When students have completed their stories, suggest that they illustrate them. Then help students create a class book, titled "Santa Fe: Oldest City of the Southwest," for their stories and pictures.

Find out more

Did you enjoy "Santa Fe: Old Town, New Town"? If so, read more about Santa Fe and the Southwest. Look for these books in your library:

- Fradlin, Dennis. *New Mexico: In Words & Pictures.* Children's Press, 1981.
- Hallett, Bill and Jane. *Look Up Look Down Look All Around Chaco Culture National Historical Park.* Look & See, 1989.
- Hillerman, Anne. *Children's Guide to Santa Fe.* Sunstone Press, 1984.

4 Before reading *"This, Too, Is Desert"*

Think of what you know

You already know many things that help you when you read. Do you know what makes a desert different from other places? Do you know if all deserts are the same? Talk about your ideas. Then write what you think this story will be about.

This selection discusses different kinds of deserts, both hot and cold, the common denominator being very little rainfall. It then explains some of the conditions that give rise to deserts, many of which are found in two bands that ring our earth on either side of the equator. The selection describes several deserts—the Sahara, North American, and polar—and points out that deserts do support plant life, especially near oases. Have students make a list of desert features on the chalkboard. Use the list to define what makes deserts different from other landforms.

Decide what you want to learn

Always read with questions in mind. Then you can look for answers to them. Look at the picture on page 122. What do you think it shows?

The photograph is of lichens growing in a desert in Antarctica.

Write one thing you hope to learn from this story.

Students may want to know how such a cold place can be a desert.

Get ready to use your reading skills

As you read, you need to put facts together. Sometimes a story does not tell how all the facts fit. The questions in the green boxes will help you. They ask you think about:

How things are alike or different. Can you compare things, events, people, or ideas to understand more about them?

What the most important idea is. Can you find a sentence that tells the most important idea of the story?

How things go together. Can you use facts and ideas you already know to help you understand new ideas?

Understand the words

Here are some words from "This, Too, Is Desert." Use the story and pictures to help you understand them.

dunes	**Fahrenheit**	**oases**	**region**
equator	**lichens**	**polar**	**temperature**

To help students with new vocabulary, have them look up the words in a dictionary and use each word in an oral sentence. You might also point out the equator and polar regions on a map or globe.

4 Reading

This, Too, Is Desert

For the question below: Life is difficult in the desert because the climate is harsh and there is little water. If students say they know of desert cities where life is not so difficult, point out that this is only because people have worked long and hard to bring in water and other things necessary for life.

Think About It

▷ Is life difficult or easy in the desert? Why?

Think of a place where the sun doesn't shine for months at a time. Cold winds blow across a land filled with ice. Only a few kinds of plants or animals can live in this cold, empty land.

Now think of a place where the temperature often goes over 100 degrees Fahrenheit. Here, sharp rocks stand hundreds of feet above a dusty plain. Small, dry bushes seem to be the only living things.

These are two very different places. Yet they are alike in one important way. Both are deserts. There are many different kinds of deserts. In fact, deserts are found all over the world. So what is it that makes a desert a desert?

Think About It

▷ What is the most important thing all deserts have in common?

All deserts have one thing in common. They are very dry. Most scientists call any place that gets 10 inches of rain a year or less a desert. One town in the Atacama Desert of Chile in South America is so dry that it has never had any rain at all.

Some deserts lie behind high mountains. Rain clouds drop most of their water before they ever reach the desert beyond the mountains. Other deserts are in places where there are hardly ever any rain clouds.

The most important thing all deserts have in common is that they are dry, mainly because there is little rainfall. Have students look for the one sentence that contains this important main idea. Then help students identify details that tell more about it.

For the question below, the sand and soil don't normally get much rain. If they did, the ground would be less hard and able to absorb water to a deeper level. The little rain that does fall either evaporates in the heat or is blown off by the wind.

Think About It

▷ What makes the desert sand and soil thirsty?

When rain does fall in a desert, it doesn't last. The hot sun soon dries the ground. Strong winds make the water run off the land. And dry sand and hard soil soak up any water, so it can't sink deep into the ground.

So deserts are places where little rain or snow falls. But where exactly do you find such dry places? Most of the world's deserts are found near two lines that circle the earth on either side of the equator. The line to the north of the equator is the Tropic of Cancer. The line to the south is the Tropic of Capricorn. The weather in these places is very dry for most of the year.

DESERTS OF THE WORLD

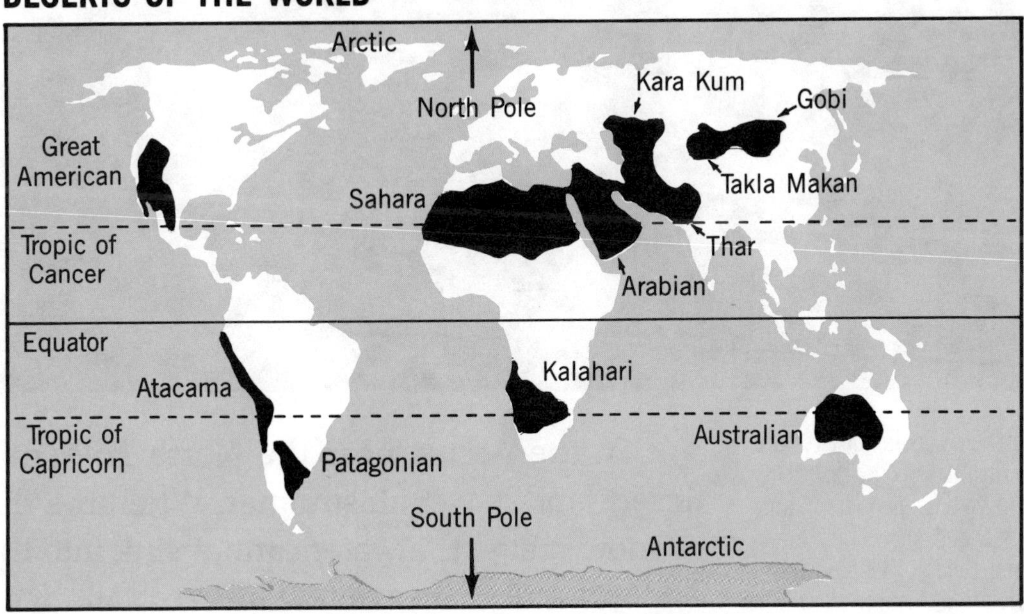

(cont.) You might demonstrate this principle by pouring water into two flower pots, one with hard-packed, dry soil (the water will run down the sides without soaking into the dirt) and the other with loose, moist soil (it will absorb water until saturated).

The largest desert in the world is the Sahara in North Africa. This one desert is almost as big as the United States! The Sahara has dry plains, high sand dunes, and mountains with snow at the top. Most of the Sahara gets less than one inch of rain each year.

Think About It

▷ Do you think it rains more than 10 inches a year in some parts of the Sahara? Why?

The United States and Mexico are home to another important desert region. The two countries share about 500,000 square miles of desert. The North American deserts are as different from each other as they are beautiful. You can see white dunes at White Sands National Monument in New Mexico. You can also see dark hills in the Black Range of Death Valley, California.

It is possible that parts of the Sahara, for example, snow-capped mountains, get more than 10 inches of rain, though most of the Sahara gets far less. Explain that the 10-inch standard is an average figure, meaning that a desert or part of a desert could get more than 10 inches of rain at some point and still be considered a desert.

Most of the earth's deserts are found near the equator. But there are also deserts in some places where you would never think to find them. Two such places are near the North and South Poles. Of course, you would expect to find a lot of ice and snow there. But there are "polar deserts" there, too. Find the North and South Poles on the map on page 123.

For the question below, polar deserts are different from other deserts in that they may be cold and wet for periods of time, and even have ice and snow. They are like other deserts, though, because they receive less water from rain or snow than most other parts of the earth. Also, water from rain and snow cannot sink into the ground because it is frozen. Point out to students that comparing things can help them better understand important ideas.

Think About It

▷ How are polar deserts different from other deserts? How are they like other deserts?

In the Arctic, near the North Pole, much of the desert land is wet all summer. When the thin blanket of snow melts, the water cannot sink into the ground. The ground is always frozen hard, all except the top few inches. So the water stays on top of the ground. The land is flat, too, so the water can't run off into rivers. Many plants grow in the wet Arctic desert in the short summer.

In the Antarctic, at the South Pole, the weather is much colder than at the North Pole. Winds are very strong. They blow all the time.

Even with the terrible weather, the Antarctic is home to plants called **lichens.** Lichens live on rocks. They break down the rocks, helping to make soil. Other plants might grow in the soil if the weather were to become warmer.

For the question below, they wait for the rain because they need water to sprout, bloom, and produce seeds. Without rain they couldn't grow.

Think About It

▷ Why do flowers wait until it rains to bloom in the desert?

The polar deserts aren't the only ones with special plants. Many kinds of flowers wait for the short desert rains before they bloom. The seeds for these flowers lie sleeping for most of the year. When the rains come, they quickly "wake up." Plants grow from the seeds, flower, and make new seeds. All this happens in just a few weeks. The flowers cover the desert in a sea of bright colors. These plants make good use of the water when it is there.

Think About It

▷ Why do you think many animals and plants are found at oases?

Many animals and plants are found at oases because there is plenty of water there to support life. Remind students that the surrounding desert is harsh and dry, which makes the oasis especially attractive to living things.

But all life does not have to fight to live in the desert. Many deserts have places called **oases.** Here large pools of water lie under the ground. Some oasis pools come up to the surface on their own. Others are brought to the surface by people. The water mixes with the soil on the ground. So beautiful trees and plants can live and grow in the desert.

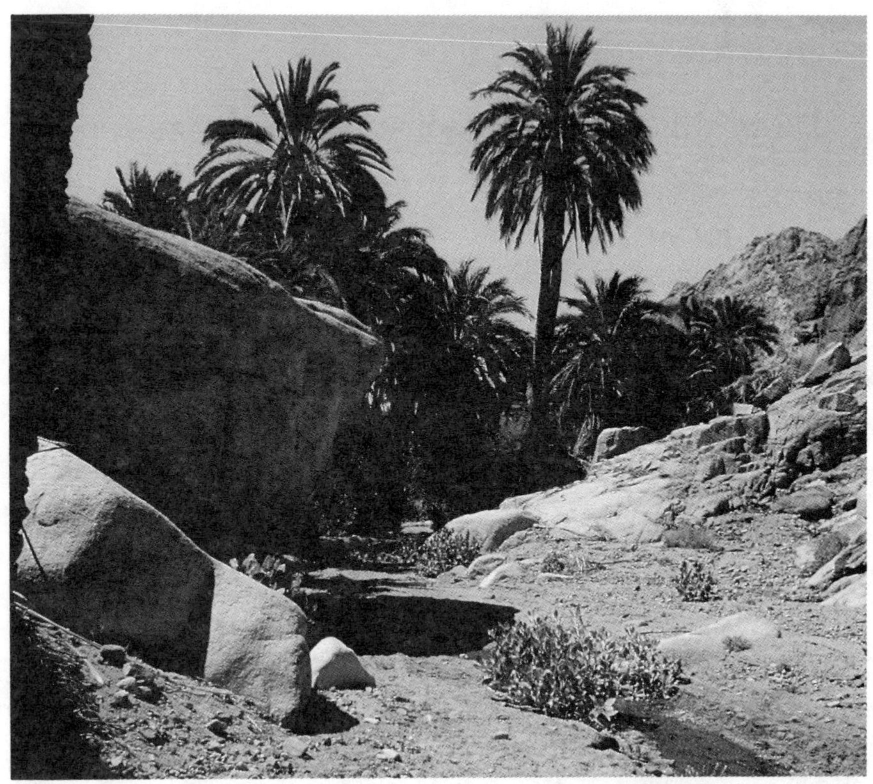

The people and animals of the deserts share the oases. They come there to drink the water and rest in the shade of the trees. Many people live in or visit the different kinds of desert land. But they almost always want to stop and rest in places that aren't quite so dry.

4 After reading *"This, Too, Is Desert"*

Think about the story

1. What kind of desert would you like to visit? Why?

Answers will vary. Make sure that students can provide appropriate reasons for their responses.

2. Do you think people should bring water to the desert to make oases? Why or why not?

Answers will vary. Some students may say that creating oases is good, since they make the land better for farming and human life. Others may say that it isn't right to create an oasis where one doesn't exist naturally, since that would bring more people to the desert and upset the natural balance for plants and animals.

3. Fill in this chart with some of the things you learned in the story.

Kind of Desert	Where It Is Found	What It Looks Like
North American	United States and Mexico	white dunes, dark hills
Sahara	North Africa	dry plains, sand dunes, snow-capped mountains
Arctic	near the North Pole	flat, frozen land, sometimes wet; plants grow in summer
Antarctic	South Pole	cold, icy, windy; lichens grow

Check what you learned

Turn back to page 121. Read again what you wanted to learn from this story. Did you find out what you wanted to know? If so, tell what you learned.

Answers will vary depending on the goals students set for themselves.

Were all your questions answered? If not, tell how you could find the answers.

Students may mention going to the library as a way to find answers to their questions. In addition, encourage students to look for some of the books suggested at the bottom of this page.

Use your own words

Pretend you are an airplane pilot flying around the world. Write about the deserts you fly over. Use a separate piece of paper and try to answer these questions:

- How can you tell when you are flying over a desert?
- Where do you see the biggest deserts?
- What colors are the different deserts you see?

Find out more

Did you enjoy "This, Too, Is Desert"? If so, read more about deserts. Look for these books in your library:

- Knight, David C. *The First Book of Deserts.* Franklin Watts, Inc., 1964.
- Leopold, A. Starker. *The Desert.* Time-Life Books, Inc., 1962.
- Rinard, Judith E. *Wonders of the Desert World.* National Geographic Society, 1976.

When students have finished the writing assignment above, encourage them to share their work with the class. You might also arrange a "revolving" display around a wall map of the world. Pin up the work of several students around the map. Then have them stretch different colored yarn from their paper to the various deserts they wrote about. Change the display each day until all students have had a chance to connect their writing to the places they wrote about.

After reading *DESERT COMMUNITIES*

Think about what you've learned

Read each question. Fill in the circle next to the best answer.

1. What are the Anasazi people best known for?
   - Ⓐ They lived long ago.
   - Ⓑ They built cliff houses.
   - Ⓒ They lived in groups.
   - Ⓓ They used water.

2. Who lived in Santa Fe during its long history?
   - Ⓐ Native Americans
   - Ⓑ Mexicans and Spaniards
   - Ⓒ Americans
   - Ⓓ All of the above

3. What is special about desert plants and animals?
   - Ⓐ their colors
   - Ⓑ their sizes
   - Ⓒ the way they use water
   - Ⓓ the way they use sunlight

4. What is true of all deserts?
   - Ⓐ They are cold.
   - Ⓑ They are hot.
   - Ⓒ They are sandy.
   - Ⓓ They are dry.

Read the question. Write your answer on the lines.

5. Look at the map on page 102. Do you think the Anasazi might have gone from Chaco Canyon to settle in Santa Fe? Why or why not?

Answers will vary. There is indeed evidence of Anasazi settlement in the Santa Fe area, and students will most likely respond in the affirmative. Make sure they provide adequate reasons for their answers.

Write about what you've learned

Deserts are changing all the time. Sometimes they grow larger. Other times they get smaller. Think of what you have read and learned about deserts. Why do you think their size changes? Write your ideas on a separate piece of paper. When students have finished their writing, encourage them to share their thoughts with the class.